# CRASH COURSE

on the

## New Testament

ΜΑΤΙΟΥΑΥΤΟΥΚΑΙ ΟΥΤΟΕΙΧΟΝ
ΟΙΗ✝ΑΝΤΟΔΙΕΣΩθ ΤΟΣΤΟ
ΑΝ ΤΟΤΕΠΡΟΣΕΡΧ ΑΝθ
ΛΙΤΩΙΥΑΠΟΙΕΡΟΣΟΛΥ
ΩΝΦΑΡΕΙΣΑΙΟΙΚΑΙ
ΑΜΜΑΤΕΙΣΛΕΓΟΝΤ
ΑΤΙΟΙΜΑθΗΤΑΙΣΟΥ
ΑΡΑΒΑΙΝΟΥΣΙΝΤ
ΑΡΑΔΟΣΙΝΤΩ
ΤΤΕΡΩΝΟΥΓΑ
ΤΑΣΧΕΙΡΑΣ
ΗΕΣθΙ
ΟΚΡΙθΕΙ
ΑΣΤΙΚΑΙ
ΙΝθ
ΤΟΥ

# CRASH COURSE

## on the

# New Testament

### SIX SESSIONS

CHRISTIANITY TODAY

INTERNATIONAL

BIBLE STUDY

Standard® PUBLISHING

*Bringing The Word to Life*

Cincinnati, Ohio

Published by Standard Publishing, Cincinnati, Ohio

www.standardpub.com

Copyright © 2008 by Christianity Today International

Editor: Brad Lewis

Creative Development Editors: Kelli B. Trujillo and Roxanne Wieman

Contributing Authors: B. Clayton Bell, Os Guinness, Joy-Elizabeth Lawrence, Jeanette Littleton, James W. Miller, JoHannah Reardon, Kristi Rector, Bruce Thielemann, F. Bryan Wilkerson, and Coy Wylie

Cover and interior design: The DesignWorks Group

All Scripture quotations, unless otherwise indicated, are taken from the HOLY BIBLE, NEW INTERNATIONAL VERSION®. NIV®. Copyright © 1973, 1978, 1984 by International Bible Society. Used by permission of Zondervan. All rights reserved. Scripture quotations marked (*NLT*) are taken from the Holy Bible, *New Living Translation*. Copyright © 1996, 2004. Used by permission of Tyndale House Publishers, Inc., Wheaton, Illinois 60189. All rights reserved.

Scripture quotations marked (*The Message*) are taken from *The Message*. Copyright © 1993, 1994, 1995, 1996, 2000, 2001, 2002 by NavPress Publishing Group. Used by permission. All rights reserved.

Scripture quotations marked (*NASB*) are taken from the *New American Standard Bible*. Copyright © 1960, 1962, 1963, 1968, 1971, 1972, 1973, 1975, 1977, 1995 by The Lockman Foundation. Used by permission. (www.Lockman.org). All rights reserved.

ISBN 978-0-7847-2247-3

14 13 12 11 10 09 08        9 8 7 6 5 4 3 2 1

# Contents

HOW TO USE THIS STUDY IN YOUR GROUP ....................... 6

NEW TESTAMENT TIME LINE ......................................... 10

1. JESUS: IDENTITY AND INFLUENCE ......................... 12

2. THE CHURCH BEGINS .......................................... 20

3. PAUL'S CONVERSION AND MISSIONARY JOURNEYS ...... 30

4. SALVATION ........................................................ 39

5. CONTROVERSIES IN THE EARLY CHURCH .................. 47

6. THE END OF THE AGE .......................................... 58

FOR FURTHER RESEARCH ......................................... 67

    Resource List ................................................. 67

    "An Efficient Gospel?" ...................................... 69

    "God's Cure for Heart Trouble" ........................... 77

    "The New Testament: Fact or Fiction?" .................. 85

# How to Use This Study in Your Group

As Christians, we are a people of the Book. We base most of our knowledge of God and our faith in God on what we read in the Bible. It's critically important that we continually take up our Bibles and pursue a greater understanding of the text and the God who is revealed through it. The goal of the Crash Course Bible Studies series is to help you and your group become more comfortable, knowledgeable, and interested in the Bible—to aid you in that great pursuit of discovering God through his written revelation.

So whether you're a brand-new Christian or a seasoned believer, whether you've read from the Bible every day of your life or are just cracking it open for the first time, you'll find in Crash Course new insights, fresh challenges, and material to facilitate dialogue.

## THE NEW TESTAMENT

In this Crash Course Bible study, you'll learn to navigate your way through the New Testament. We are going to explore what we need to know about this story, and how God wants to use his story to change our lives. The

New Testament is the story of Jesus and the early church. The New Testament should not be interpreted apart from the Old Testament; it's a fulfillment of God's story that began with creation. And in this study, we'll see how the two are intimately connected and interwoven.

We'll see how Jesus has played a role in the world from creation to now. We'll also discover how the early church was born—and how it survived intense pressure, persecution, and controversy. We'll take a look at the role of the Holy Spirit in the lives of the early believers and in our lives now. This is the continued story of God's people: a people he loved so much that he sent his only Son as a sacrifice to redeem them. This is the story of the birth of Christianity, the fulfillment of the Old Testament, and the promise of God's kingdom to come.

## ABOUT THE SESSIONS

Each session in this book is designed for group use—either in a small group setting or adult Sunday school class. The sessions contain enough material to keep your group busy for a full ninety-minute small group time but can also be easily adapted to work in a shorter meeting time—a true crash course. Or if you'd like to spend even more time, feel free to take two weeks for each of the six sessions; that essentially provides a quarter of a year's worth of content for your group.

The readings, activities, and discussion questions will help your group dig deeper into the Bible passages, engage in thought-provoking dialogue, explore ways to personally apply the material . . . and get to know one another better! Every group member should have a copy of *Crash Course on the New Testament*, both for at-home readings and for use during group time. As you go through the study during your group time, take turns reading aloud the text and questions in the book. That gives everyone a sense of participating in the study together.

Here's how each session breaks down:

## Launch

At the beginning of each session, you'll find a great introduction to the topic (be sure to read this aloud at the beginning of your meeting!), a list of Scriptures you'll study during the session, any extra supplies to bring, and notes on anything else to prepare before the session.

There's also a launching activity to start your group time. This activity sets the stage for the week's topic and gets people ready to start talking!

## Explore

Next up is the meat of the study—the "Explore" section. This portion includes several teaching points that each focus on a specific aspect of the broader session topic. As you explore each teaching point, you'll study some Scripture passages, interact with one another as you talk through challenging questions, and read commentary on the passages. Also included are excerpts from related Christianity Today International articles (more about that below) that will enrich group discussion. If you are leading the group, be sure to ask God to help you make his Word come alive for your group during this time of exploring his truth (see Hebrews 4:12).

## Apply

The Christian life—the abundant life—is about more than just thoughtful study and dialogue. James says, "As the body without the spirit is dead, so faith without deeds is dead" (James 2:26). The "Apply" section of each session will help take your discussion and study to another level; it will help you *live out* the ideas and values from that session. During this time, each participant will choose from three different challenge options (or come up with their own) to do during the coming week. These challenges will help group members make what they've learned a part of their lives in a practical way.

### Pray

Before you finish up, be sure to take some time to pray for one another. In the "Pray" section, you'll find an idea you can use for your group's closing prayer.

### Before Next Time

Take a look at the "Before Next Time" box for a heads-up on what to read or prepare for your next meeting.

# FOR FURTHER RESEARCH

### Resource List

Located at the end of session 6 is a list of recommended resources that can help take your study on the topic even further. You'll want to check those out!

### Christianity Today International Articles

You'll also find three bonus articles from Christianity Today International publications. These articles are written by men well versed in the New Testament. The sessions reference the articles during the course of the study. These articles are meant to help your group dive deeply into the topic and discuss a variety of facts, thoughts, and opinions. Taking the time to read these articles (as well as anything else suggested in the "Before Next Time" box at the end of each session) will greatly enrich your group's discussion and help you engage further with each topic.

It's our prayer that *Crash Course on the New Testament* will change the lives of your group members as you come to better understand the New Testament and our God and Savior who is revealed there. May the Holy Spirit move in and through your group as you study the New Testament and seek to live out its timeless messages.

# New Testament Time Line

## 430 BC–6 BC

- After Malachi, God sent no more prophets to his people until he sent John the Baptist.
- The Jewish people were scattered all over the known world, teaching others about the true God, establishing synagogues, and translating the Old Testament into the Greek language of that day to make it accessible to Jews and non-Jews alike.

## 6 BC–AD 8

- When the time was right and when God's preparations were complete, Jesus was born in Bethlehem, fled to Egypt with Mary and Joseph, and returned to live out his childhood in Nazareth.

## AD 26–AD 30

- Jesus' baptism and temptation
- The calling and sending of the Twelve
- Teaching illustrated by miraculous signs
- The transfiguration in which the divine nature of Jesus was dramatically revealed to three of his disciples.
- The final week of Jesus' life on earth including the triumphal entry into Jerusalem, the Last Supper, and Jesus' death, burial, and resurrection.

## AD 30–AD 45

- The coming of the Holy Spirit at Pentecost
- The early church in Jerusalem sharing all things in common
- Early persecution by the Jews, including the first martyr, Stephen
- Conversion of Saul of Tarsus (Paul)
- The church spreads into Judea, Samaria, and to the Gentile lands north of Israel

ΙΗ†ΑΝΤΟΔΙΕ<ω°°ΠΟΓΕΥΟΜΕΝΟΝ

## AD 45—AD 60

- The gospel is preached throughout the Roman Empire by Paul and his companions during three missionary journeys.
- Paul writes letters to churches in Rome, Galatia, Corinth, and Thessalonica while on these journeys.
- James, the brother of Jesus, leads the church in Jerusalem and authors a letter to Jewish believers.

## AD 55—AD 68

- Paul is arrested in Jerusalem and is imprisoned in Jerusalem, Caesarea, and Rome, awaiting trial before Caesar.
- Paul writes letters to churches in Ephesus, Philippi, and Colosse and a personal letter to Philemon of Colosse during this first period of imprisonment.
- Eyewitnesses to Jesus' ministry, John Mark and Matthew, write the Gospels bearing their names. Paul's companion and personal physician, Luke, does extensive research on the life of Jesus and the early days of the church and writes the Gospel of Luke and the book of Acts.
- Paul is released from prison, then later is rearrested.
- Paul writes his letters to young evangelists Timothy and Titus.
- Peter and Jude (another brother of Jesus) write letters to churches in Asia fearing persecution and fighting false teaching. Hebrews was written to Jewish Christians considering returning to Judaism in the face of possible persecution.
- Paul, Peter, and many other Christians suffer death during the brutal regime of Nero.

## AD 90—AD 95

- John remains as the only surviving member of Jesus' twelve disciples and ministers in the Asia Minor area.
- John authors the Gospel bearing his name, retelling the story of Jesus centered upon seven miraculous signs of Jesus rather than the chronology used by Matthew, Mark, and Luke. John focused upon the facts that he witnessed, revealing Jesus to be both fully human and fully divine.
- John authors three letters to the churches in the Asia Minor area, refuting false teaching that questioned the humanity and divinity of Jesus.
- John was exiled to Patmos, a small island off the coast of Asia Minor.
- While on Patmos, John received a vision from Jesus that he recorded in the book of Revelation.

# Jesus: Identity and Influence | 1

Answering Jesus' question, "Who do you say I am?"

*Most of us live in history for a certain segment of time. We arrive and live our estimated seventy-year life span. If we're really effective humans, our influence might live on another decade or two after we're gone. What a contrast to Jesus! His ministry didn't begin with what we celebrate as Christmas morning. And it didn't end when his thirty-three years on earth were finished.*

*In this study, we'll explore the life of this one who lived out a plan from the beginning of time . . . a plan that's still ongoing and will continue until the end of time. Why did Jesus come to earth? What's he all about? And how does his plan for us continue? We'll discuss some of these basic questions.*

ΙΗϯΛΝΤΟΔΙΕϹШΟΝΠΟΓΕΥΟΜΕΝΟΝ

BIBLE BASIS: *Genesis 1:1-5; Isaiah 53; Mark 8:27-29; John 1:1-14, 19-34; 10:22-38; 14:15-31; Romans 8:9, 10; Ephesians 1:3-23; Colossians 1:15-20; Hebrews 3:1-6; 4:14-16*

EXTRA SUPPLIES: *pens, white board and markers (or paper and tape), 3 x 5 index cards*

BEFOREHAND: *Since this is the first week of your study, the leader should send out an e-mail to everyone in the group. Remind them to purchase their copy of* Crash Course on the New Testament *if they haven't already. Encourage group members to read the articles "An Efficient Gospel?" by Tim Keel on page 69 and "God's Cure for Heart Trouble" by Greg Laurie on page 77 in preparation for this week's session. Be sure to mention where and when you're meeting.*

 # LAUNCH

In Mark 8:29, Jesus asked his disciples, "Who do you say I am?"

That's a question we're going to look at today.

The Old Testament, New Testament, and even our culture use many words to describe Jesus. Different groups of people have viewed Jesus in different ways, and those different descriptions often reflect different perspectives on his life, identity, and mission.

Break into groups of two or three and think of several terms that describe Jesus. These can be words or phrases that you believe or that you've heard others say, such as *Messiah, great teacher, Son of God,* or even *liar.* One member of each smaller group should write the terms on a white board (or on paper and tape them to the wall)—so the larger group can see all. In your smaller groups, take some time to discuss these questions:

Why do you think so many differing opinions of Jesus exist?

What one term best sums up for you who Jesus is? Why?

 EXPLORE

*Teaching Point One: Jesus' existence started long before his time on earth.*
*Read Genesis 1:1-5; John 1:1-14 and Colossians 1:15-20.*

When we look at who Jesus is, one fascinating and hard-to-comprehend truth is that he wasn't just a figure in one era of history. In a sense, he *is* history. The first verses of the Bible might be some of the best-known words from the Old Testament. But Scripture tells us much more about who created the world. In his Gospel, the apostle John tells us that "all things were made" through the Word (referring to Jesus; John 1:3). The Word later became a human, meaning that he serves as the bridge that allows us to become God's children. This takes place, as the apostle Paul says, "by making peace through his blood, shed on the cross" (Colossians 1:20).

While you personally have never seen Jesus in a physical sense, how does knowing that he lived as a human provide some connection to him?




Why do you think God the Son, rather than God the Father or the Holy Spirit, came to dwell most closely with humans on a tangible, visible level?

In "An Efficient Gospel?" Tim Keel writes, "Every articulation of the gospel I'd heard focused exclusively on Jesus Christ and his role as redeemer. Of course, it's true and good news that Jesus and his life and work function redemptively. But when we reduce Jesus to redeemer only, we miss another essential element of our faith: that Jesus is also creator" (p. 75).

Reread John 1:1-14 and consider Keel's words. How does thinking of Jesus as your creator change the way you view him? How does it influence your perspective of him as Redeemer and Savior?

*Teaching Point Two: We must ask ourselves, "Who do I say Jesus is?"*
*Read Isaiah 53; Mark 8:27-29; John 1:19-34 and 10:22-38.*

Jesus pointedly asked his disciples, "Who do you say I am?" The answers given by the disciples and others in Scripture have shaped history. This is one of the most important questions we will ever answer.

What did Jesus' disciples think about who Jesus was? What did they expect from him?

What are some of the ways Jesus is described by Isaiah (Isaiah 53)? by John the Baptist (John 1:19-34)? by Jesus himself (John 10:22-38)?

"Who do you say I am?" What a huge question! But it's also a question we need to break down and answer every day. More important than your words is the way you show your answer: by how you prioritize your time and activities, by the way you treat others, and by the choices you make each day. From the passages above, answer Jesus' question for yourself: "Who do you say I am?" How are you living out that answer?

## Teaching Point Three: Jesus' existence is eternal.
### Read John 14:15-31.

In a sense, the Jewish leaders—and at times even the disciples—seemed to try to put Jesus in a box. But before we point a finger at their narrow-mindedness, we need to think of how we often do the same thing. For example, sometimes we think of Jesus only as our Savior, who died for our sins. However, his importance doesn't end there—or begin there.

How do these verses reveal Jesus' role after his death? How has he played this role in your life?

The disciples were *with* Jesus; they had the chance to listen to him, touch him, ask him questions. Unfortunately, we've never experienced Jesus *in the flesh* as they did. What makes Jesus feel real to you even though you've never seen him? When do you feel far from Jesus? How does what he says here help you?

In "God's Cure for Heart Trouble," Greg Laurie points out: "The disciples didn't understand that Jesus came to this earth with the express purpose of going to the cross, dying for the sin of the world, and then rising from the dead. They thought he would establish an earthly kingdom. When he said, 'I'm going to leave you,' it freaked them out. That's why Jesus went on to say, 'Do not let your hearts be troubled.' Essentially, he was saying: 'Even when it seems like your world is falling apart and darkness is going to overtake you, you don't need to feel anxious or worried'" (p. 78).

Reread Laurie's last sentence there. How is Jesus a comfort when your world is falling apart? Why is it about more than an earthly kingdom? How does that knowledge help you when things are rough here?

### Read Romans 8:9, 10; Ephesians 1:3-23; Hebrews 3:1-6 and 4:14-16.

Jesus' role in our lives continues, both now and throughout eternity. He serves as our high priest, meaning we can approach him with the problems and pressures of life, knowing he will meet us with his divine wisdom, power, and undeserved spiritual blessings.

Based on these passages, list some of Jesus' roles now and in the future. How do these roles affect you?

Which roles do you easily allow Jesus to play in your life, and in which roles do you resist his authority? Why do you think that is?

What steps can you take to hand Jesus ownership of those roles in your life?

How do the descriptions of who Jesus is and the eternal roles he plays surprise you? Which do you want to think more about after you leave your group's meeting today?

 APPLY

What new aspects of Jesus have you seen in the Scripture passages and discussion today? What descriptions of Jesus can you add to your list from the "Launch" time? Add any new ideas to the others on the board (or paper on the wall). Not only can Jesus be your personal Savior, he also wants to be your friend. He knows and loves you personally. He was a member of your Creation Team. In fact, even if you were the only person alive who sinned, Jesus would have come to earth and died for you. And he's preparing a place for you to live eternally with him.

Look at the words you've used to describe Jesus. Which ones best describe the roles Jesus plays in your life right now? Which words describe a role you'd *like* Jesus to play in your life? Write down those words on an index card so you can reflect this week on what Jesus means in your life.

In addition, choose one of the following application options to do on your own this week. Turn to a partner and share your choice.

### JESUS ON CANVAS

Take time out of your normal schedule to do some artwork. You can use pens and paper or a cloth banner, a computer graphics program, paint on a

ΙΗ†ΑΝΤΟΔΙΕCꟿᴼᴴΠΟͰΕΥΟΜΕΝΟΝ

piece of glass, or any other format you choose. Create a poster or collage using names and descriptions of Jesus. Be as elaborate or simple as you like. You can create your artwork alone or ask family members to help. If you want, you can bring your creation to the next session.

## MORE ABOUT JESUS

Choose at least one of the words or phrases you've used to describe Jesus and his roles. Using a Bible concordance or www.biblegateway.com, look up Scriptures pertaining to that name or role. For example, if you want to learn more about Jesus as counselor, look up words like *counselor* and *guide.*

## REMEMBER BRACELET

Use alphabet beads and elastic thread or leather cord to make a bracelet that spells out a name or role of Jesus, such as Redeemer. Wear the bracelet to remind you of the ways in which Jesus fulfills that role in your life. If you don't want to wear alphabet beads, you can use a permanent marker to write a name or role of Jesus on a wide rubber band and wear that.

 # PRAY

Use an open roundtable prayer style for your closing prayer time. The leader can start the prayer, and others who want to thank Jesus for his different roles can pray too. Use this prayer time to focus just on Jesus.

---

BEFORE NEXT TIME: *Read "The New Testament: Fact or Fiction?" by Steve May on page 85 to prepare for next week's session.*

---

# *The Church Begins* | 2

Empowered by the Holy Spirit, the early church spread rapidly—even in the midst of trials and persecution.

*The events that took place during the beginnings of the early church aren't just exciting historical tales. The actions of the first apostles as they embraced and spread the message of Christ—and particularly as the Holy Spirit empowered their actions—also made the present-day church what it is now. As the apostles took the gospel across ethnic and national boundaries, the trials they experienced only seemed to increase their zeal. Their stories can inspire us in many ways—as we experience the Holy Spirit empowering our ministries, as we live in community within our churches, as we face persecution and grow in boldness through our trials, and as we live out our faith in both the everyday and dramatic events of life.*

BIBLE BASIS: *Psalm 73:23-28; Acts 1:1-9; 2:1-4, 38-47; 4:23-37; 5:12-42; 16:16-34; Romans 8:18; 2 Corinthians 4:16, 17; Philippians 1:29*

EXTRA SUPPLIES: *pens and paper, a copy of* The Message *Bible*

BEFOREHAND: *As group members arrive, the leader should receive any artwork brought by those who did the "Jesus on Canvas" option from last week. Display the art and decide on an appropriate time during the session to comment on it. The leader should also alert a good reader to help out during "Pray."*

 # LAUNCH

Break into groups of three or four people. Make sure that each group has pens and paper. In these small groups, make a list of all the ways you try to maintain or increase your physical health: diets, exercise regimens, vitamin supplements, special equipment you've used, regular physical exams, etc. Be as specific as you can. Then spend a few minutes discussing the following questions:

What successes or failures have you experienced in trying to stay healthy or even increase your overall physical health? What rewards or benefits have you experienced?

As Christians, what do you think we need to do to be *spiritually* healthy? Can you think of ways God helps us be more spiritually fit?

# EXPLORE

*Teaching Point One: The Holy Spirit dwells in Jesus' disciples.*
*Read Acts 1:1-9.*

As the Christian faith was just beginning, Jesus knew exactly what his disciples needed. He supplied that need—the Holy Spirit, whom Jesus called "the gift my Father promised" (v. 4). Jesus knew the disciples needed more than just human enthusiasm; they needed to be filled with the Holy Spirit. Without his power they couldn't begin to do the job of spreading the good news of the gospel "to the ends of the earth" (v. 8).

Why did Jesus use the word *baptized* when he spoke of the Holy Spirit? What do you think being "baptized with the Holy Spirit" symbolized?

What did the disciples' question, "Lord, are you at this time going to restore the kingdom to Israel?" (v. 6), demonstrate about their understanding of the future? How did Christ's answer and his ascension affect that perspective?

*Read Acts 2:1-4.*

What do you think the elements "violent wind" and "tongues of fire" symbolized? Why is it significant that so many international Jews were there (and could understand the disciples in their own languages)?

How does the Holy Spirit give us power today? How have you experienced the power of the Holy Spirit in your own life?

### Teaching Point Two: The early church is an example of beautiful Christian fellowship.
### Read Acts 2:38-47 and 4:32-37.

After the Holy Spirit came and empowered the apostles, Peter addressed the crowd that had gathered. While Scripture doesn't state how many people heard Peter speak, it does say that three thousand people repented and were baptized that day.

This was the first church! They met in the courts of the existing Jewish temple. They experienced fellowship as they ate together in one another's homes. They even sold their possessions and gave the proceeds to others in need. As a result, more and more people became Christians each day.

List some practical ways this first church practiced its faith. How did these "exercises" make the early Christians spiritually healthy? What exercises can you apply from these passages to become more spiritually healthy?

What appeals to you about the way the early church lived out its faith?

How does the first church compare to churches today? to your church? What are some ways you'd like to see your church become more like the early church? What can you do to help your church accomplish this?

**Teaching Point Three: The early church was persecuted for its faith. Read Acts 5:12-42.**

The first church grew and prospered for a while, but it wasn't long before the disciples and the first Christians ran into people who didn't like what they were doing. Yet even as these early Christians faced persecution, their trials ultimately led to the spread of the message of Christ to far-flung parts of the known world. The main question that confronted the first believers is one that we all must face even today: If we know trials, suffering, and persecution will come, will we still confidently stand up for our faith and tell others about Jesus?

What most stands out to you in Acts 5?

Look at Peter and the other apostles' statement in 5:29-32. Why do you think it made the members of the Jewish council so mad?

The apostles were flogged and ordered "not to speak in the name of Jesus" (v. 40). It has been said that this was like ordering the sun not to shine.

They didn't stop. What drove them to such lengths of personal suffering and martyrdom?

Read the section "It Has Passed the Test of Time" in the article "The New Testament: Fact or Fiction?" (p. 89) by Steve May. How would you answer for yourself the "main question" from the previous page? Even if you know that trials, suffering, and persecution will come, will you still confidently stand up for your faith and tell others about Jesus?

How can you find comfort and courage in Gamaliel's words (vv. 38, 39)? How does Steve May's argument in his article echo Gamaliel's words? Does this argument resonate with you? Why or why not?

## Read Acts 16:16-34.

Things started well for Paul and his colleagues as he ministered in the city of Philippi. But then he confronted the demon in the slave girl. Tired of the demonic interruptions, not wanting to have any allegiance with the devil, and in compassion for the girl, Paul said to the demon, "In the name of Jesus Christ I command you to come out of her!" (v. 18). It did, at that moment. When the Roman authorities found out that Paul and his companions were Jews, the situation went from bad to worse. They accused Paul's party of subverting Roman law, and immediately commanded them to be severely beaten and imprisoned.

Humiliated, stripped, and beaten, Paul and company prayed. In fact, they did more than pray! With an attitude of worship and adoration, they praised God in their prayer—even with their backs bleeding and their feet in stocks. Because of their worship, God prompted some surprising and miraculous events to occur.

What purpose do you think singing and worshiping served? Read Psalm 73:23-28. How has God sustained you during trouble and suffering?

If you had just been publicly humiliated, stripped, beaten, and placed in stocks in the recesses of a dark prison, what would you pray? Would you praise and worship God? Or would you ask, "Lord, why did you allow this to happen to me? What did I do wrong? Don't you care about me?" Why do you think Paul and Silas were able to accept what had happened and to praise God in the midst of it?

Have you ever seen surprising or even miraculous events as a result of your suffering? Share your experience with the group.

Remembering the suffering Paul went through during this experience, read the following verses that Paul wrote and discuss the accompanying questions.

Romans 8:18: What reason is given for being patient in suffering? Why can we go even a step further and thank God for our present trials?

2 Corinthians 4:16, 17: How can we be inwardly renewed? Paul suffered a great deal, yet he called his troubles "light and momentary." Why?

Philippians 1:29: Why does Paul make suffering sound as though it's a privilege? When have you experienced suffering or persecution? How do you feel about that experience? How has it affected your faith?

## APPLY

The early church didn't begin because a group of people got together and said, "Let's start a church" or, "Let's throw together a new religion." Instead, the church began and expanded because the apostles took the teachings and actions of Jesus and taught and acted just as he did. Empowered by the Holy Spirit, they overcame trials, suffering, and persecution—boldly living out their faith. As we follow in their footsteps some two thousand years later, we can know the same blessings that come from standing up for our faith and boldly telling others about Jesus.

Choose one of the following application options to do on your own this week. Turn to a partner and share your choice.

## VISIT A CEMETERY

A lot of people plan out their lives very carefully. Career, marriage, two kids, and a dog. Three bedrooms, two baths, and a two-car garage. An adequate retirement plan. Yet they all end up in the same place, and you're standing in it. Be respectful during your visit, and perhaps find a quiet spot under a tree near the gravestones. Spend some time in prayer, asking God if he has something in mind for you instead of or in addition to the usual plan. Ask him to show you the ways he wants you to share the message of the gospel in spite of any trials, suffering, or persecution that may come. Before you leave, write down one action or step you sense God is guiding you to take.

## OUTSIDE YOURSELF

Look through current newspapers, magazines, and online news sources. Find a story of someone who has suffered a tragedy or difficulty. If you were face-to-face with that person, how would you advise him or her to praise God in spite of the situation? Now think through a recent tragic or difficult time in your own life. How can you take your own advice?

## START A "CHURCH"

Talk to several people you know about starting a gathering of Christians. This isn't meant to replace your regular church gathering, and it can be any kind of group: a workplace prayer group, a Christian book club, a stay-at-home moms' encouragement group, a dinner fellowship group, or anything else you can create. Be open to occasionally inviting non-Christians to your group. From what you've studied about the first Christians, make a list of the ways God works through ordinary faithful people to carry out his plans. Together, choose one or two of these ways and put them into practice.

 PRAY

Have a group member with an expressive reading style read aloud Acts 4:23-35 from *The Message* version of the Bible. This passage begins with "As soon as Peter and John were let go" and concludes with "according to each person's need."

As you listen, spend time in silent prayer, asking God to place in your heart the courageous attitude and faith of the first Christians. Your prayers might echo some of the vivid phrases in this passage: that you'll experience "wonderful harmony" with other Christians; that you'll have "fearless confidence" when speaking God's Word and telling others about Jesus; that you'll be of "one heart" and "one mind" with other Christians, and so on.

---

BEFORE NEXT TIME: *Read "An Efficient Gospel?" by Tim Keel on page 69 to prepare for next week's session. The leader should plan to bring some images of relatively modern people who generally are considered evil, such as Adolph Hitler, Osama bin Laden, and Timothy McVeigh. Clip pictures from magazines or newspapers, or print them from the Internet.*

# Paul's Conversion and Missionary Journeys | 3

The "apostle to the Gentiles"
advances the spread of the gospel.

Next to Jesus Christ, the apostle Paul is likely the most influential person in the New Testament. Most scholars agree that he wrote nearly half the books of the New Testament, and his writings address many practical aspects of living a Christian life.

Prior to his conversion, however, Paul (once known as Saul) was zealous in his persecution of Christians. According to Acts 8:3, "Saul began to destroy the church. Going from house to house, he dragged off men and women and put them in prison." However, on the road to Damascus—where he planned to hunt down Christians and take them back to Jerusalem to prison—Saul experienced a dramatic conversion to the very faith of which he'd been an enemy. After his conversion, he began to preach the message of Jesus almost immediately.

*Calling himself "the apostle to the Gentiles" (Romans 11:13), Paul traveled increasingly greater distances from Jerusalem on three missionary journeys around the Roman Empire. In addition, he traveled to Rome as a prisoner. From his dramatic conversion to his influence on many early churches, Paul played a central role in the formation and history of Christianity.*

---

BIBLE BASIS: *Acts 1:8; 7:55–8:3; 9:1-28; 14:26–15:21; 16:16-40; 17:16-34; 20:13-37*

EXTRA SUPPLIES: *pictures of people considered evil*

BEFOREHAND: *The leader should put the pictures in a central place where everyone can see them.*

---

# LAUNCH

Look at the pictures of "evil" people. Briefly share what you know about each person, and then discuss the following questions:

How would you feel if you found out one of these people had become a Christian and started preaching the gospel?

Would this person's past actions make you more or less likely to want to hear and believe what he was saying about God? Why?

# EXPLORE

*Teaching Point One: Saul passionately persecuted the early believers.*
*Read Acts 7:55–8:3.*

Saul was a passionate man who lived out his convictions. Early in his life he was known for his hatred and persecution of people who followed Jesus. He threatened them and even helped carry out their deaths. If you were a Christian, you didn't want to see Saul headed your way! What do you think drove Saul to such lengths in his persecution of Christians?

When have you treated others poorly based on your preconceived notions about them? How did you feel afterward?

Describe a time when your beliefs were challenged and you came to appreciate or support a different point of view. How has that experience changed you?

*Teaching Point Two: Saul experienced a dramatic and miraculous conversion—and redemption.*
*Read Acts 9:1-28.*

When Saul traveled to Damascus—where he planned to arrest Christians and bring them to Jerusalem for trial—he experienced a dramatic conversion in his beliefs through an encounter with Jesus. From that moment, Saul's passion changed from hating Christians to proclaiming Christ—even under persecution.

How would you have felt if you'd been asked to accept Saul into your home—and been told he'd converted? Why did Ananias and Barnabas accept Saul? What role did other Christians play in Saul's transformation?

How does Saul's conversion demonstrate the depths of Jesus' redemptive power? How has this given you hope in your own life—and for those you love?

If you became a Christian as an adult, how has your life changed since you became a Christian? How has God redeemed your past and used it for good?

If you feel comfortable, briefly share about your life before you met Jesus and how knowing him has changed you.

### Teaching Point Three: Paul dedicated his life to spreading the message of Jesus.

The Holy Spirit commissioned Paul to preach the gospel, and the apostle took three major missionary journeys throughout the Mediterranean, spreading the message of Jesus to Jews and particularly to Gentiles (non-Jews). Letters Paul wrote to churches that he visited and established on these journeys have become books of the Bible, such as Ephesians, Galatians, Philippians, 1 and 2 Corinthians. During Paul's mission trips, he experienced some of the persecution he had doled out to Christians before his conversion. He was chased, beaten, stoned, jailed, brought to court, and more for preaching the gospel. But in spite of these hardships, he continued his missionary work, with God leading the way through promised protection and the help of other believers.

Break up into three smaller groups, numbered one to three. In your respective groups, read the passage assigned to your team and discuss the three questions.

### Group 1: Acts 14:26–15:21

- Paul spent much of his missionary career preaching to Gentiles. Why do you think God chose Paul to preach to the Gentiles?
- What obstacles did the Gentiles face in the early church?
- Is there a group of people in today's world that you would compare with the Gentiles of the early church? In what specific ways can we reach out to that group of people?

### Group 2: Acts 16:16-40

- How did Paul and Silas respond to their incarceration and persecution? What gave them the strength to stay so positive?
- What do you make of Paul's compassion toward the jailer? How did that affect the jailer? his family?
- What can we learn from Paul's actions in this passage?

### Group 3: Acts 17:16-34

- What's significant about the dynamics of this group that Paul preached to in Athens?
- How did Paul make the gospel clear and relevant to this group?
- What can we learn from Paul's approach to evangelism in this passage?

After about ten minutes in the smaller groups, come back together as a large group. Choose one spokesperson from each smaller team to briefly report on the Scripture passage and what was discussed.

### Read Acts 20:13-37.

According to Luke, the writer of the book of Acts, what activities did Paul undertake during his trips?

Look carefully at the quoted words of Paul (vv. 18-35). How would you feel if he spoke these words directly to you, phrases like "keep watch over yourselves," "men will arise and distort the truth," and "I commit you to God"?

Why do you think God chose a person like Paul to be one of his greatest instruments in spreading the gospel?

### Read Acts 1:8.

Jesus spoke these words to his disciples right before he ascended into Heaven. Where were Jesus' disciples instructed to witness (to tell people) about him? What is the significance of those places?

How did Paul later apply these words to his sharing of the gospel?

What do these words mean for us today as we share our faith?

 APPLY

During his preaching and missionary journeys, Paul addressed issues that Jews and Gentiles were dealing with in their lives, and brought Jesus to them. Our mission today isn't really any different. In Tim Keel's article "An Efficient Gospel?" read the section "A Gospel You Can Live With" and through the third paragraph of the next section "Rich and Robust Revolution" (p. 72).

Consider our response to Paul's conversion and missionary journeys. How can we encourage other believers when they struggle to live out their faith in today's postmodern world of stress, diversity, and moral relativity?

Discuss with the group: How can we bring the truth of the gospel to people around us in ways that meet them where they are? Answer the same question in a more personal way: How can *you* bring the truth of the gospel to people around *you* in ways that meet them where they are?

Choose one of the following options to make this week's study of Paul's life more personal to you.

## WRITE YOUR STORY

Write or outline the story of how you came to faith in Christ. Follow the example of Paul in the book of Acts by describing your life before you came to know Jesus, how you came to believe and give your life to him, and how your life has been different since. The process of thinking through and writing down your personal conversion story will help you share it with others. Be bold and ask God to give you opportunities to share your story and to show people how God is relevant and active in our world today.

## WRITE A LETTER

Use one of Paul's examples to write a letter to another Christian. Remind that person of God's promises, describe the ways you're praying for him or her, and encourage the person to continue to live as Christ would want.

## MAP IT

Find a map of the United States. Where have you traveled? If you have gone overseas, also find a world map. (If you don't have copies of these maps already, do an online search for printable maps.) Use a highlighter to trace from your starting point to the places you've traveled. How have you been a messenger of God's kingdom in those places? Pray and ask God to open your eyes to the ways you can spread the good news wherever you go; and pray that God would soften your heart to the needs of his people around you.

# PRAY

Have each person in your group pray for the person to the left. Pray for one another: that God would give you the boldness of Paul to share your faith, and that you would each be a witness to others through your words and actions every day. Take turns praying aloud so each person can be encouraged by the prayers of other group members. If your group is large, break up into smaller groups of three to four people to pray this way.

BEFORE NEXT TIME: *In the spirit of Paul encouraging the churches he visited, the leader should send each group member a brief e-mail of encouragement this week. Mention something specific that you're praying for, such as a work problem mentioned at the meeting or a family situation you know about. The leader will want to gather (or assign someone to gather) the extra supplies needed for next week's "Launch" activity—and may want to save session time by preselecting and cutting out the images indicated in the activity. Everyone should read (or at least skim) the book of Romans to prepare for next week's session.*

# *Salvation* | 4

*At its core, salvation is simple. Brief verses in Scripture sum up the whole message of salvation. Verses like John 3:16, 17: "For God so loved the world that he gave his one and only Son, that whoever believes in him shall not perish but have eternal life. For God did not send his Son into the world to condemn the world, but to save the world through him." Verses like Romans 3:22, 23: "This righteousness from God comes through faith in Jesus Christ to all who believe. There is no difference, for all have sinned and fall short of the glory of God."*

*However, in the book of Romans, the apostle Paul describes the wonderfully rich and textured process of living out our salvation. He focuses not just on the term* salvation, *but deftly weaves in the related theological concepts of justification, sanctification, and transformation.*

ΟΥΚΛΙΕΣΕΛΘΩΝΕΚΕΙΟΕΝΦΛΟΝΕ

BIBLE BASIS: *John 3:16, 17; Romans 3:9-31; 5:1-11; 6:1-14; 8:1-17*

EXTRA SUPPLIES: *old magazines and newspapers (or images already cut out) for the "Launch" activity, colored pencils or markers, scissors, glue or tape, construction paper*

BEFOREHAND: *Arrange some work areas for the "Launch" activity.*

# LAUNCH

You've received invitations to parties before. Sometimes people go all out on the look of the invitation; other people simply send e-mails. If God wanted to invite us to receive his gift of salvation, what do you think his invitation might look like? Using images from magazines and newspapers, colored pencils or markers, and a sheet of construction paper, design your own mock-up of an "invitation to salvation." It doesn't have to be anything fancy or professional—it just needs to express in some way what you think this invitation would look like. Take about ten minutes, and then share your invitation with the group. Explain why you put your invitation together the way you did.

# EXPLORE

*Teaching Point One: Justification is total and complete—it's God's gift to us through Jesus.*
*Read Romans 3:9-31 and 5:1-11.*

The message of the gospel begins with some bad news: that we're all sinners. According to Romans 3:10, 11 not even one person is righteous. Of course, this doesn't mean we're as bad as we can possibly be. Most of us try to be good people, but being sinners means we are infected with sin, like a body with a virus. This infection affects our minds and our hearts, causing us to do the wrong thing instead of the right thing, to be self-centered rather than others-centered, to do things our way instead of God's way. Even when we try our best to fight this virus, we don't always win. Inevitably, at times we fail.

We're all infected with sin, and it creates all kinds of problems for us. It separates us from God, one another, and our true selves. Ultimately, that separation leads to death—physical and spiritual death. That's bad news. However, justification fills us with hope by freeing us from our past lives as sinners. Romans 5:8 tells us, "While we were still sinners, Christ died for us." And Romans 3:22-24 says, "This righteousness from God comes through faith in Jesus Christ to all who believe. There is no difference, for all have sinned and fall short of the glory of God, and are justified freely by his grace through the redemption that came by Christ Jesus." Justice was done at the cross, allowing a just God to accept all who put their faith in Jesus.

That's justification: the act of God declaring righteous the repentant sinner who turns in faith to Christ. If you've done that, then God has nothing against you—no record of your wrongs, no permanent record of your failures.

In your own words how would you define *justification*?

Why is it so important to recognize that everyone is a sinner and no one is righteous?

Romans 5:1 states that justification gives us peace with God. How does it do that?

Why was Christ's death necessary? What is your reaction to Christ's sacrifice? Try to put your emotions into words.

Reread Romans 5:8. How does this verse reassure you of God's love for you? How does it make you feel? How does his love motivate you?

### Teaching Point Two: Sanctification is a daily pursuit of holiness.
### Read Romans 6:1-14.

Justification is a one-time act, but sanctification is a daily decision that you commit to for life. In justification, God declares you to be a righteous person. In sanctification, God develops you into a righteous person day by day. It's explained on www.bibletruths.net as follows: "The Greek word translated 'sanctification' (*hagiasmos*) means 'holiness.' To sanctify, therefore, means 'to make holy.'"

The great news is that sanctification is God's work, not just ours. He gives us his Holy Spirit to guide and empower us through each step of growth. What does the new life God wants for us look like?

In what ways are you still a slave to sin? Or are you?

How could thinking of yourself as "dead to sin" help you be free of sin? How does being under grace instead of the law help you conquer sin?

Have you had any disappointments in your Christian life—anything you wanted to see change but didn't? Why do you think that was the case?

What does it mean to come alive to God? What changes about you?

### Teaching Point Three: Transformation is the work of the Holy Spirit. Read Romans 8:1-17.

God wants to transform everything about us, from the inside out. He wants to transform you from the person you are into the person he created you to be. What will it take for us to become the people God wants us to be? In a sense, transformation takes the daily process of sanctification and makes it permanent. But doing this takes some outside help. More accurately, it takes some *inside* help. Making our transformation complete—so that we actually become new people and live new lives—requires the work of the Holy Spirit. Paul certainly understood the role and work of the Holy Spirit, mentioning him nineteen times in Romans 8 alone!

Why is it so hard to just follow the rules and do what's right?

In what ways do you still feel in bondage to sin? What will it take for you to be free?

What do you think it means that we "do not live according to the sinful nature but according to the Spirit" (v. 4)?

In what ways do we let our sinful nature control us? Why is the sinful mind hostile to God? How can we let the Holy Spirit control our minds instead?

How can you know whether or not the Holy Spirit is living in you?

How has the Spirit transformed you? Use words that express your emotions and feelings.

## APPLY

When we dig deeper into the meaning of salvation, it can be difficult to study theological terms like *justification, sanctification,* and *transformation* and still keep it feeling personal and relevant. Yet that's exactly what salvation is!

Salvation involves your repentance—asking God to forgive your sins. And salvation also involves your own faith—believing that Jesus died for your sins, believing that God raised him from the dead, confessing with your own mouth and your actions that "Jesus is Lord," and identifying yourself with his death and resurrection in Christian baptism.

Choose one of the following application options to do on your own this week. Turn to a partner and share your choice.

## SIN CONQUEROR

In 2 Corinthians 12:7-10 Paul describes "a thorn in my flesh." Some commentators believe this "thorn" was an actual physical ailment. But some believe it was a tormenting temptation. Is there a constant sin in your life—something that you just can't seem to conquer? If so, spend some time in prayer, asking God to be strong in your weakness—to help you defeat your sin through the power of the Holy Spirit. Pray that God would continually renew your mind so you are focused on him and his kingdom instead of on the sin that keeps you in chains.

## OUT WITH THE OLD

Spend some time thinking about one thing you'd like to change about yourself. Maybe you need to get rid of a bad habit. Perhaps you need to change a behavior that keeps you away from God. You might even need to suspend or end relationships that you realize cause you to sin. Write down a brief description of what you'd like to change. Then tear the paper into shreds to symbolize your willingness to renounce that sin. Ask God to make the change in your life just as drastic and complete as destroying the paper. If you're comfortable sharing some details, call or e-mail to ask some of your group to pray for you to experience continued victory over that area.

## EXTREME MAKEOVER

You've probably seen the popular TV show that completely refurbishes a needy family's home in a week. The result is often a makeover of the family's life too. Think about what we've discussed today. If you had an opportunity to make over your life in a way that you think would truly please God, what would that look like? Draw, use images from magazines or newspapers to create a collage, sculpt with modeling clay, or use any medium you like. The idea isn't to create an image that looks like you, but rather one that visually represents the priorities and focus of your life—were you to live as a transformed person.

 # PRAY

We started this session by stating that while salvation includes the process of justification, sanctification, and transformation, at its core the message of salvation is simple. Close your time together in an attitude of prayer. Pray something like this: "Jesus, we believe you were our substitute—the one who paid our debt—when you died on the cross. Even if we don't fully comprehend it all, we believe that you shed your blood, died, were buried, and rose again for us. God, we thank you for forgiving our sins. Show us areas of our lives that you want us to change, old behaviors or habits we need to stop and new ones we need to start. Make clear for us those times when we need to turn away from our old ways and run straight into your loving arms."

---

BEFORE NEXT TIME: *Spend a few minutes reviewing "An Efficient Gospel?" by Tim Keel on page 69 before your next session.*

---

Conflicts resolved by the first Christians show how we
can settle disagreements in our churches today.

The Bible doesn't hide the fact that the early church had difficulty
agreeing about certain beliefs. If we're saved through grace, why do
our actions still matter? Was Christianity just for Jews, or could
Gentiles also be believers? And when Gentiles became Christians,
did they need to follow traditional Jewish laws? We shouldn't be
surprised at the disagreements the early church faced. Like a newly
formed extended family, these early Christians had to learn to
deal with their conflicts. At the same time, they learned to respect,
understand, and love each other—even when they disagreed!

Thankfully, the teachings of the apostles cleared up many of these
conflicts. In fact, these teachings provide both comfort and a practical
model for facing conflict in the church today. Let's look at some of the
controversies, and at how early church leaders found resolution and

*remained united around the main goal of spreading the message of the gospel. Through their example, we can learn the value of relationships with fellow believers who are different than we are, but who stretch and challenge us to love one another—even when we disagree.*

---

BIBLE BASIS: *Acts 10:24-48; 15:1-21; Romans 6:15-18; 1 Corinthians 8:1-13; Galatians 1:6-17; 3:1-5; Ephesians 4:1-16*

EXTRA SUPPLIES: *timer or stopwatch, pens and paper, white board and markers (or large sheets of paper and tape)*

---

 LAUNCH

Controversies are nothing new to humanity. To learn of some controversies in the early church, read the fourth paragraph under "A Gospel You Can Live With" in Tim Keel's article "An Efficient Gospel?" (p. 72). Break into groups of three and discuss the next two questions.

Why do you think these controversies arose in the early church? How do you think these conflicts threatened the unity of the early church?

Now set a timer for five minutes. In your groups of three, try to list as many controversies within contemporary Christianity as you can think of. You might list both theological and lifestyle disagreements, such as interpretations of Scripture, varying worship styles, the celebration of Halloween, or drinking alcohol. Once the timer rings, stop brainstorming. Look at your list and discuss how you feel about these conflicts and controversies.

ΙΗ✝ΑΝΤΟΔΙΕΣΩᴼᴴΠΟᵣΕΥΟΜΕΝΟΝ

Why do you think these controversies exist? Even in this group, is there disagreement on which are matters of Bible truth and which are matters of conscience? How do these conflicts threaten the unity of the church?

While many important controversies revolve around matters of Bible truth (which should not be compromised), more seem to revolve around matters of conscience or opinion. Today's session will deal mostly with this second group, the kind of controversies that we need to be more flexible and tolerant about.

 EXPLORE

*Teaching Point One: Many of the church's first controversies involved the gap between Jews and Gentiles.*
*Read Acts 10:24-48.*

Peter traveled to Caesarea because of a dream he had and after Cornelius invited him to his home. This was a big deal because Peter was Jewish and Cornelius was a Gentile. Jews didn't associate with Gentiles at this time and especially wouldn't enter their homes, because Gentiles ate (or in the language of the Jews, "defiled themselves with") foods that Jewish law prohibited. By entering a defiled person's home, a Jew could easily become defiled as well. However, God showed Peter that the gospel was for all people, not just the Jews.

From this passage, list instances when a cultural norm was breached or something unexpected happened. What can these kinds of events tell us about the way God works?

Imagine going into a type of place that, for moral reasons, you'd never entered before. For Peter, this was the home of a Gentile. For you, it might be going to the red-light district or attending a ritual in a Buddhist temple. How would a similar situation make you feel? Can you imagine a situation when God would ever ask you to do that? Why or why not?

If you truly believed that God wanted you to go to a place that would normally be outside your comfort zone, would you go? Or would you stop because of peer pressure—what fellow Christians might think? Explain.

*Read Acts 15:1-21.*

As Jewish followers of Jesus began to let go of Old Testament law requirements and traditions (such as mandatory circumcision and food laws) that they'd previously assumed to be required for people joining their community, they struggled to understand the balance between salvation through grace and obedience to God in love. *Was it necessary*, they wondered, *for Gentile believers to also follow the law?* The apostle Paul addressed this question in Romans 6, and the apostles and leaders of the early church tackled it here, in Acts 15.

Read Peter's speech (vv. 7-11) aloud. What do you think he means by the phrase "a yoke that neither we nor our fathers have been able to bear"?

ΙΗΤΑΝΤΟΔΙΕϹѠ°ᴴΠΟΓΕΥΟΜΕΝΟΝ

What sort of conclusion did these leaders come to at the end of the passage? Read Romans 6:15-18. How does Paul's statement here relate to the decision the church council made in Acts 15?

When have your beliefs about an issue conflicted with those of a fellow Christian? Did you and the other person resolve the conflict? If so, how? When you and another Christian disagree about an issue, do you need to always reach an agreement; or is agreeing to disagree an acceptable solution? Explain your answers.

### Read 1 Corinthians 8:1-6.

In Paul's first letter to the Corinthian church, he responded to a question asked in a previous letter. The church wondered whether they should eat meat sacrificed to idols or not. In the first century, Greek and other pagan temples served multiple purposes. While Greek temples served as places to worship Greek idols, they also functioned as the primary sources of acquiring meat. No corner butchers or supermarket delis existed in those days. To our contemporary ears, it seems like early Christians could easily avoid the choice to eat meat sacrificed to idols, but they couldn't. If they wanted to eat meat, it had probably been sacrificed to an idol at a temple. And if they wanted to eat out with friends, they would head to a restaurant-like setting at the local temple.

How does Paul describe the relationship between knowledge and love? Why do you think he links these concepts to answer whether these Christians should eat meat sacrificed to idols?

In your own experience, what controversies or disagreements with others required both knowledge and love to resolve? How did you use each? Which is your usual go-to in an argument—knowledge or love? How can you learn to balance both?

**Teaching Point Two: Sometimes the attitude of those involved matters more than the controversy.**
*Read 1 Corinthians 8:7-13.*

As Paul answered the Corinthian Christians' question about eating meat sacrificed to idols, he recapped the two opposing arguments. Some claimed that because the idols didn't exist and God created everything, it was OK to eat the meat. But others loathed the idea of importing elements from their former lifestyle into their new life in Christ. Do you think Paul took sides in this passage—pointing to either group as being right or wrong? Explain.

What do you think this controversy was really about: food or Christian identity? Why?

Paul's solution involved not allowing the freedom we have in Christ to become a stumbling block to others. Or to put it simply: Eating meat sacrificed to idols isn't the real problem; offending/confusing/tempting other Christians is.

As a group, list some actions that are controversial among Christians today—some believers have no problem with them, others think of them as sin. Here are a few to get you started: watching R-rated movies, drinking alcohol, dancing. Note the actions on a board (or large sheet of paper taped to the wall).

Why do you think people argue over whether or not these actions are OK? What behavior or action do you personally have no problem with, but that bothers a fellow Christian? According to this passage, how should you handle this situation? In what ways is this challenging for you?

*Read Ephesians 4:1-16.*

Sometimes we tend to see things only as they relate to us. But Paul challenged those who follow Jesus to avoid this kind of me-centered vision. Instead we need to see a broad view of how things affect the whole.

Think through the gifts and roles Paul described in this passage. Which do you have or fulfill? How have you used your gifts in the past? How do those gifts give you a sense of unity and purpose within your church? How can that sense of unity and purpose help you resolve—or avoid—conflict in your church?

*Teaching Point Three: Run the good race.*
*Read Galatians 1:6-17 and 3:1-5.*

Paul wrote to the Galatians about some of the controversies we've already looked at. "Some people" in their congregation were teaching that in order to experience full salvation, the Gentile Christians needed to be circumcised. Paul wrote the church to convince them not to listen to these false teachers. "You were running a good race," he wrote. "Who cut in on you and kept you from obeying the truth?" (5:7).

The false teachers claimed that "Jesus plus something else" was required in order to have salvation in Christ. Describe an experience when someone claimed that your personal relationship with Christ required "Jesus plus something else." How did you respond?

Some controversies of the early church seem to have little to do with us today. Few Christians now argue that we must follow Jewish law, most churches teach salvation by grace (not works), and we don't head to temples to buy meat sacrificed to idols.

However, one of the similarities between all the conscience-related controversies we've considered today is that each requires a cultural shift in the minds of believers. At first, the idea of visiting the home of a Gentile appalled Peter. And why not? His entire life revolved around the idea of staying pure and not defiling himself. Going to a Gentile's home was exactly that: defilement. The way of Christ was new, foreign, and decidedly uncomfortable. And that's not much different from what most of us face today.

Controversies have always been part of the church, whether it's inerrancy of the Scripture, slavery, women's roles, the deity of Jesus, divorce, sexual behavior . . . What good things have resulted from these and other controversies? What bad things have resulted? How have some of these controversies required a cultural shift for Christians?

What current controversies do you think will shape the future church in a big way?

How can Christians engage in a controversy and maintain unity at the same time?

For you personally, when does taking a stand on an issue seem like a good thing to do? When does maintaining unity and neutrality seem like the right thing to do? Explain.

## APPLY

How amazing is it that God's inspired Word includes accounts of controversies, conflict, and troubles in relationships among believers? God certainly doesn't hide the truth that when people get together there's bound to be conflict. Fortunately, God also provides plenty of guidance in Scripture to help us work through our conflicts and disagreements.

Choose one of the following application options to do on your own this week. Turn to a partner and share your choice.

### TAKE AND EAT

Read Acts 10:1-23. In this passage, God prepared Peter to do something that he previously considered wrong. Reflect on and write down ways God prepared you or changed your heart to do something you were unsure about. What purpose do you think he had in mind? How did you decide it was OK? What Scripture might have helped? If this hasn't happened to you, consider how God might use you in a foreign or uncomfortable situation. As a symbol of your willingness, eat a foreign or highly unusual food that you usually wouldn't taste.

## FROM THE OTHER SIDE

This week, listen to or read something different than you usually do. For example, if you typically listen to news coverage with a certain political slant, try finding a source that provides a different perspective. How does this feel? How can you evaluate the material objectively? How can this experience help you to better understand friends, coworkers, or neighbors?

## REACH OUT

Is there a neighbor, coworker, or fellow Christian whom you often disagree with? Think about your relationship with this person in light of what we've studied today. If you feel prompted by the Holy Spirit, contact this person this week. Take a moment to chat, or suggest that the two of you go out for coffee. How can the ways the early church managed controversy influence your relationship with each other? How can you change even if the other person doesn't?

 # PRAY

Whether church controversies center on matters of conscience or matters of Bible truth, hurt and division are often the result. Briefly mention some of the contemporary controversies you've listed during this session, with the idea of asking God to bring knowledge and wisdom as well as healing and unity in those areas. End your study by reading the following prayer together, based on Romans 15:5, 6: "May the God who gives endurance and encouragement give us a spirit of unity among ourselves as we follow Christ Jesus, so that with one heart and mouth we may glorify the God and Father of our Lord Jesus Christ."

---

BEFORE NEXT TIME: *For the next session everyone should try to bring one cultural point of reference to the book of Revelation. These might include books, DVDs, and other references to the end times. Review "God's Cure for Heart Trouble" by Greg Laurie on page 77 to prepare for the next session. For the leader: Reading and studying the book of Revelation can be a daunting task. The book's author, the apostle John, uses vivid imagery and unfamiliar metaphors to describe the vision that God revealed to him. To help members of the group better understand the passages they'll be studying, bring a Revelation commentary to the session. To save session time, look up the "Bible Basis" passages from Revelation ahead of time and highlight some key comments you'd like to feature.*

# The End of the Age | 6

God's promised kingdom provides a glorious vision
of what lies ahead for his followers.

The end of the world has been a topic of interest throughout history. Similarly, the way that God will bring about the end of time—as told in the mysterious and ominous book of Revelation—has been a curiosity throughout church history. The vivid descriptions of Revelation threaten a violent judgment of the world, yet promise believers hopeful visions of what is to come. The book isn't meant to be a script for cheesy horror movies; it's a letter from an exiled pastor encouraging his congregation to persevere through intense suffering as they wait for the fulfillment of God's coming kingdom. For Christians today, it provides a metanarrative of history—a bird's-eye view—showing us that God will one day overthrow the corrupt kingdoms of this world and establish his own kingdom once and for all.

ΙΗΥ ΑΝΤΟΔΙΕΘΩ⁰ʰ ΠΟΡΕΥΟΜΕΝΟΝ

BIBLE BASIS: *Isaiah 40:10, 11; Daniel 7:9, 10; Revelation 1:9-16; 3:14-22; 4:1–5:10; 5:12, 13; 10:1-3; 21:1-8*

EXTRA SUPPLIES: *Bible commentary on the book of Revelation (highlighted by the leader), cultural points of reference to Revelation*

BEFOREHAND: *A couple of early arrivers should look over the notes the leader has highlighted in the Revelation commentary and be prepared to read those at the appropriate times during the study.*

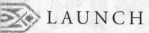

# LAUNCH

Display the contemporary cultural points of reference to the book of Revelation that members brought (books, DVDs, and other references to the end times). As you look at the items collected, discuss the following questions. If your group is large, break into groups of four or five people for this discussion.

- What do you think the average person on the street who doesn't profess to be a Christian would think about the items we've brought?
- Why do you think the book of Revelation receives so much attention in the public sphere, even among people who don't read the Bible?
- What gut-level feelings do you have about the book of Revelation?

# EXPLORE

*Teaching Point One: Revelation is full of powerful and symbolic images. Read Revelation 1:9-16.*

Revelation, a book filled with strange yet significant images, was written by the apostle John. This disciple of Jesus, who had served as a leader in the church in Ephesus, was exiled to the island of Patmos while the Roman Empire persecuted his church. God revealed to John a series of images promising that God would bring justice to the world and deliver the persecuted church.

While we can easily be confused by the images John used in this book, spend some time dissecting this passage. Consider the "loud voice like a trumpet"; the "seven golden lampstands"; the descriptions of the Son of Man ("robe reaching down to his feet," "golden sash," "head and hair . . . white like wool," "eyes . . . like blazing fire"); the "seven stars" held in his right hand; and the "sharp double-edged sword." What do you think the various images represent?

What words here arouse emotions? What words of comfort do you see in this passage?

## Read Daniel 7:9, 10.

Many of the images representing God in Revelation are similar to the images of God in the book of Daniel, a prophetic book that describes a time when God's people were persecuted by the Babylonian and Medo-Persian Empires that ruled over them. Just as Daniel had been thrown into the lions' den (Daniel 6), the Romans during John's time began to throw Christians to the lions in their theaters. How might this similar language from the book of Daniel and John's vision comfort the persecuted people of John's church?

***Teaching Point Two: Revelation has much to say about worshiping God alone.***
***Read Revelation 3:14-22.***

Revelation 2, 3 contains a series of letters to seven churches of Asia Minor. In these, God revealed to John the things that pleased and displeased him about each of those churches—sometimes comforting them, sometimes challenging them. This particular letter, addressed to the church in a city called Laodicea that was known for its wealth, addressed the subject of their riches and encouraged them to seek spiritual riches. It referred to images that would have been familiar to them. Laodicea was known for its medical school and for the black wool garments made there.

Why might God be concerned about the moral purity of this city? What did this have to do with their persecution and suffering?

Reread 3:17, 18. Why do you think John told these wealthy people that they were "wretched, pitiful, poor, blind and naked"? What do you think each of the items he urged them to buy in verse 18 implies?

John was concerned that his people maintain their faith and values in the face of huge challenges. In his article "God's Cure for Heart Trouble," Greg Laurie explains why confident faith carries us through crises and stress. Read the section titled "Trust We're Going to Heaven" (p. 80).

In what ways are we like those in the church in Laodicea? Maybe you've never thought of yourself as rich, so you don't seek the trappings of wealth. What do we seek rather than seeking God?

*Teaching Point Three: Jesus is the Lion and the Lamb.*
*Read Revelation 4:1–5:10.*

We might think of this text as the center of the book of Revelation. It begins by inviting us to look through a doorway into Heaven, to see how things really are in the universe. Despite the claims of those who persecuted them, the early Christians could believe that God was still in charge.

Some Bible scholars believe that the four living creatures (4:6-9) represent four constellations in the sky. What do you think these creatures might symbolize? What does this say about the entire world worshiping Jesus as Lord and king?

Some of the Caesars who ruled over Rome demanded that the people worship them as gods. It's sometimes tempting to worship or revere something tangible in the here and now. We don't have Caesars demanding our worship, but what tangible and earthly things or people do we worship in place of God? Why is it so tempting to worship them?

Why is it so critical (and comforting) to remember that God is on the throne (and in control)—even when you're suffering?

In Revelation 5:5, 6 John presents Jesus as both the Lion and the Lamb. As the Lamb, he became the sacrifice who took away the sins of the world. John said the Lamb appeared to have been "slain," meaning that Jesus still bore the marks of his sacrificial death. As the Lion, Jesus is the judge who punishes his enemies (2 Timothy 4:1). In Revelation 10:1-3 a "mighty angel" (either Jesus or his representative) holds a scroll containing impending judgments. He has power and authority, and calls out with a "loud shout like the roar of a lion."

How can it affect us if we see Jesus as just the Lamb or just the Lion? Why do you think we need to see these two characteristics in balance?

Read Isaiah 40:10, 11. How does it make you feel to know that the "LORD comes with power" to judge the world? How does it make you feel to know that he will gather his lambs and hold them "close to his heart"?

As you think of your eternal destiny and the eternal destinies of those you love, how can Jesus' impending judgment give you a sense of urgency and purpose? What actions does this make you want to take?

*Read Revelation 21:1-8.*

This passage is one of the great promises in Scripture. It guarantees that the land that God's people have always hoped for—the "new Jerusalem"—will finally come. At that time, God and humanity will finally be united and there will no longer be sadness. Jesus refers to himself as "the Beginning and the End." *Arche*, the Greek word for *beginning*, literally means the one who starts things off, like an architect. *Telos*, the Greek word for *end*, refers to the way things are designed to be in the end, like a blueprint. Jesus is literally the architect who designs the world in the beginning and also the model for what we are to look like when he's done with us.

What does it mean for you to know that Jesus is shaping you into his own likeness?

What images stand out to you in this passage?

How does it change your life to realize that you're on the way to a final place of peace?

 APPLY

Revelation doesn't have to be scary, nor can it be dismissed as fantasy. Instead, Revelation sounds a clear call for us to worship our God with a sense of purpose and urgency! In reverence and adoration, we can echo the innumerable angels who sing: "Worthy is the Lamb, who was slain, to receive power and wealth and wisdom and strength and honor and glory and praise! . . . To him who sits on the throne and to the Lamb be praise and honor and glory and power, for ever and ever!" (Revelation 5:12, 13).

Choose one of the following application options to do on your own this week. Mention your choice to someone else.

### HOW WILL IT END?

Read Robert Frost's poem "Fire and Ice" (one online source is www.poem hunter.com). Write down what you think he's saying about human nature and the end of the world. Compare it to what Revelation says about the end of the world. Note how Revelation compares to most doomsday stories and predictions about the end of the world.

### PACKED AND READY TO GO

Make a list of the things you pack and plan when you go on vacation. Come up with the categories that you always consider (such as clothes and toiletries, and also things like sightseeing or rest). Now make a list of how we ought to plan for eternity. Try to use some of the same categories. What would you need to have prepared? What do you hope to see?

### DEMYTHOLOGIZING HEAVEN

Find stereotypical images online or in print of what many people think of when they refer to Heaven. Using an online site such as www.biblegateway.com, see if you can find a biblical basis for them. If they don't seem to come from the Bible, where do you think they come from? Read Revelation 21. What do you think we can know about Heaven? Using images from magazines, pens and paper, or a computer graphics program, create your own image of what you think Heaven might be like.

## PRAY

Think about how much time you spend planning for a vacation. Now think about how much time you spend planning for eternity. Pray through a list of things for which you need God's help in order to be ready for eternity. Then spend some time praising God for preparing an eternal home for you.

---

BEFORE NEXT TIME: *Because this is the final study session in* Crash Course on the New Testament, *the group might want to meet once more for fellowship and food and to spend time together celebrating the completion of this course. Members could scan the six sessions in this book before the get-together in order to find the most meaningful or life-changing thing they've gained from your study together. Then close the celebration with group members sharing that personal point. In addition, if your group plans to continue studying together, consider what Bible subject you want to tackle next. If you like the approach of this Crash Course study, check out www.standardpub.com for other titles in the series.*

---

ΙΗ✝ΑΝΤΟΔΙΕϹⲰᵒᴴΠΟΓΕΥΟΜΕΝΟΝ

# FOR FURTHER RESEARCH

Note: The Crash Course series is designed to help you study important topics easily. The following magazine articles and books present additional valuable research. Items in the resource list are provided as a starting point for digging even deeper. Not everything in "For Further Research" is necessarily written from a conservative evangelical viewpoint. Great discussion and real learning happen when a variety of perspectives are examined in light of Scripture. We recommend that you keep a concordance and Bible dictionary nearby to enable you to quickly find Bible answers to any questions.

## RESOURCE LIST

*101 Amazing Truths about Jesus That You Probably Didn't Know*, Mark Littleton (Howard Books, 2007). Fascinating facts about Christ for new and seasoned believers.

*The Case for the Real Jesus: A Journalist Investigates Current Attacks on the Identity of Christ*, Lee Strobel (Zondervan, 2007). An atheist-turned-Christian focuses on rediscovering the real Jesus, whose identity and message have come under attack in recent years.

*The Life and Ministry of Jesus: the Gospels* (New Testament, Volume One in the Standard Reference Library, Standard Publishing, 2007). A through-the-Bible commentary that takes the reader from the manger to the empty tomb. Carefully weaving the details from all four Gospels into a single thread, the book gives a wonderful sense of the story of Jesus' life.

*The New Testament Church: Acts–Revelation* (New Testament, Volume Two in the Standard Reference Library, Standard Publishing, 2007). A through-the-Bible commentary that takes the reader from Pentecost to Patmos. This book chronicles the phenomenal growth of the early church, then looks at the epistles written to help that church grow and handle the challenges of confronting a pagan culture.

*The Message of Acts: The Spirit, the Church, and the World*, John R. W. Stott (InterVarsity, 1994). This book explores the early days of the church as recorded in the book of Acts, and examines what the experiences of the early church have to say about issues that concern Christians today.

*To Live Is Christ: Embracing the Passion of Paul*, Beth Moore (B & H Publishing Group, 2001). Broken into fifty short bites, this book provides a biblical overview of Paul's life from his conversion to his ministry and martyrdom.

*Paul, A Novel*, Walter Wangerin Jr. (Zondervan, 2001). For a different take on Bible study, try this novel based on Paul's life in Scripture, filled in with fictionalized accounts.

*The God Conversation: Using Stories and Illustrations to Explain Your Faith*, J. P. Moreland and Tim Muehlhoff (InterVarsity Press, 2007). When you want to tell others about God's gift of salvation, why not simply have a conversation? This book can help you use stories as illustrations with spiritual applications. In addition, the book contains dozens of short and well-written stories, with frequent sidebars giving deeper understanding to the applications.

*The Nature of the Atonement: Four Views*, edited by James Beilby and Paul R. Eddy (IVP Academic, 2006). This is a scholarly introduction to views on atonement, with each contributor responding to the others' essays.

*Revelation: Four Views: A Parallel Commentary*, Steve Gregg (Thomas Nelson, 1997). Provides summaries of four traditional views of Revelation in parallel columns, along with information about commentators on Revelation throughout church history.

*Breaking the Code: Understanding the Book of Revelation*, Bruce Metzger (Abingdon Press, 2006). Offering solid scholarship but in a nonacademic style, this book helps readers discern God's message in Revelation by exploring passages of great beauty and comfort and those that seem bizarre, bewildering, and even frightening.

# An Efficient Gospel?

*The modern world was inclined toward reduction,
efficiency, and things you can count.*

by Tim Keel

I'd been a disciple of Jesus Christ for less than a year when I first heard "the gospel question." It was May 1988, and I was spending the summer following my freshmen year of college working as a counselor at a Christian sports camp in the Missouri Ozarks. As counselors, we arrived a week before the campers showed up for a week of preparation and training. After long days of physical labor, we gathered in the evening to worship and listen to teaching designed to prepare us to lead the campers both toward God and athletic excellence. The topics ranged from end-times prophecies to prayer, and sex and dating to evangelism and discipleship—all in the context of learning to throw a tight spiral, land a back handspring, or field a grounder.

One night, the camp director stood before several hundred of us and asked the gospel question. Not the proverbial, "If you were to die tonight, do you know for sure where you'd spend eternity?" Instead he said, "If someone were to ask you what the gospel is, what would you say?"

The question caught me off-guard. I had no idea. And suddenly I was nervous. I think I knew that the first four books of the New Testament were called the Gospels. I remember that gospel meant "good news," and that the good news was about Jesus Christ. As a new believer, I was smitten by Jesus. I'd surrendered my life totally to Jesus and seized every opportunity to grow and be obedient to God. But that night, for the first time, I heard "the gospel" referred to as an entity unto itself. It seemed to have a definition distinct from the melded concepts of God, Jesus, the church, and everything I thought I understood. Not only did I have to admit that I had no idea what "the gospel" was, I also had to grapple with the fact that I wasn't even sure what our leader was asking.

Over the next few years, I came to understand the nature of the question I heard on that summer night. More than that, I learned what the right answer was supposed to be. At my university, I discovered that "gospel" was a word many Christians used as shorthand for explaining the message of salvation in a simple and efficient way.

The gospel essentially was a series of propositions meant to "save" someone. When these propositions were followed logically and sequentially—and then accepted as truth by faith—the subject could be certain of his or her eternal destiny: heaven after death. But as I've continued in my faith and in ministry, I've continued to struggle with "the gospel question." I still wrestle with what's being asked and how it has been answered. I'm not alone. Many of us want to be faithful to Jesus, and we seek to be faithful to a broader and deeper Christian tradition than the one that evolved in America after World War II.

In many ways, this quest comes down to the question I heard sitting on a gym floor 20 years ago: "What is the gospel?"

If we ask, "Is our gospel too small?" we imply that something is off kilter—that somehow we've gone off course in the way we answer "the gospel question." But it might not be just our gospel that's too small. It might be that we've been living in a world that was too small—the small, reduced world of modernity.

One of the features of the modern world was "reductionism": the belief that complex things can always be reduced to simpler or more fundamental things. To reduce something means taking it out of context and taking it apart. Church leaders have become experts at reductionism. Ministries that experience success in one context are reduced to "models" that we try to duplicate in other contexts. Sometimes such reductionism is effective. But when we use reductionism indiscriminately, we end up in a world so simplified that we barely recognize it.

So in a modern world, we tend to reduce the complexity and diversity of the Scriptures to simple systems, even when our systems flatten the diversity and integrity of the biblical witness. We reduce our sermons to consumer messages that reduce God to a resource that helps the individual secure a reduced version of the abundant life Jesus promised (John 10:10). And the gospel itself gets reduced to a simplified framework of a few easily memorized steps.

As you might guess by now, if that's what is meant by gospel, then yes indeed, I believe our gospel is too small.

I don't know how you interpret statements like this, but I can tell you what it's like to write them. It's scary. It seems dangerous to say such things these days. Everyone appears to be on their theological guard (which also tells us something about the reduced nature of our gospel). Those of us who raise questions about our gospel being too small find that our questions provoke fear—and when people are frightened, hospitality is often the first casualty.

In the absence of hospitality, we Christians are in danger of balkanizing ourselves. In the power vacuum that resulted in Eastern Europe when the modern empire of the Soviet Union dissolved, previously unified states were the scene of bitter wars fought to stake out homelands of ethnic or religious purity. To balkanize now means to divide—by increasingly precise means of differentiation—one place, one thing, one idea, or one group of people from another.

As modernity's hold on us weakens, life is being balkanized. Whether it's actual physical territory, the battle-torn terrain of the culture wars, or the polarized environment of political rhetoric, we've never been so aware of our differences. Often in the church, our theological discourse and territorial disputes are no different. The impulse to create sovereign mini-states cleansed of perceived cultural and theological enemies often seems unavoidable.

## A GOSPEL YOU CAN LIVE WITH

However, we're not the first followers of Christ to struggle with our understanding of the scope and scale of the good news. Indeed, we believe that "the Word became flesh" (John 1:14): God revealed himself in a specific time, in a specific place, among a specific people. Jesus came to the world in the form of a man to join a story in progress. God entered and engaged. And this is the calling of the church as well—to join in and participate in God's story at work in the world—in our time and in our spaces.

The gospel must become incarnate. It's something that must be lived. We cannot approach God or the gospel a-contextually.

In the New Testament, we find the early church in a very similar situation—a colony of the kingdom of God contending for their new faith and struggling profoundly to understand the implications of the birth, life, death, and resurrection of Jesus Christ. Talk about having to reorient your theological imagination!

Circumcision or no circumcision? Meat sacrificed to idols or no meat sacrificed to idols? Sabbath observance or no Sabbath observance? Gentiles or no Gentiles? The church constantly had to reframe its theology in response to the reality of Jesus and his Spirit being alive in the world. The church constantly contended for the faith—and not just with their adversaries, but with one another. So one consistent theme in all Paul's letters is the necessity of unity. Yet as they contend and struggle along, they do so in a locally responsive way that generates life and engagement with the issues of their time, culture, and geography.

This engagement is no less critical for us than it was for them. Just as the early, largely Jewish church was forced to reckon with the Gentiles' response to their witness, so the emerging world is forcing the church to reckon with the gospel in ways that it hasn't had to in a long time. Recent books like Robert Wuthnow's *After the Baby-Boomers* and David Kinnaman and Gabe Lyon's *unChristian* are helping us discover that we live among postmodern people who embrace mystery, diversity, and complexity. Yet often our "evangelism" instinctively aims to convert them first to a modern worldview, then to Jesus.

## RICH AND ROBUST REVOLUTION

Are there signs of life emerging that point towards a more holistic and robust answer to the gospel question than I heard 20 years ago? Where is the Holy Spirit forcing his people to reckon with the scope of God's work in the world, to once again consider the nature and scope of the gospel?

As I listen to the "gentiles" coming to faith in my own setting, I'm discovering that the version of "the gospel" I was given as a college-age counselor was largely missing the earthly, communal, and social nature of what God has been about since the beginning of salvation history. First with Israel, then with the church, God has animated a people to enact his saving way of life as a prophetic witness against, and a hopeful alternative to, the destructive narratives of the surrounding world.

In God's alternative reality, no aspect of our lives exists outside the scope of God's salvation and purposes. Salvation isn't just "then and there"; it's also "here and now." What's more, churches aren't just collections of individuals who will one day be reunited as souls in God's presence. God's life starts and is available to people in the present—and heaven is understood to be that place where God's rule and reign are active among his people.

Jesus says, "Wake up! The kingdom of God is at hand" (Mark 1:15, author's paraphrase). Do we speak with this kind of confidence and hope in our proclamation? Has our articulation—and more importantly, our embodiment—of the gospel invited people to become a part of an alternative reality, a community of salvation for this world and the world that is yet to come?

And here's the encouraging news: when Christians proclaim this richer gospel, the "gentiles" around us are intrigued.

A socially progressive journalist named Zack Exley has been documenting a massive cultural shift that is happening among young, theologically conservative evangelicals. Writing for the left-leaning, semi-socialist magazine *In These Times*, Exley has chronicled his journey into the surprising world of socially conscious, justice-oriented evangelicals who are living out their faith in increasingly radical and sacrificial ways. In his article "Preaching Revolution" (complete with a Che Guevara-ized portrait of Jesus on the red magazine cover), Exley wrote:

> Recently, I blogged a series of essays titled "The Revolution Misses You" in which I called for progressives to revive the forgotten dream of practical yet radical change. Friends and colleagues immediately scolded me for using "extreme" terms such as "revolution" and "radical." "You'll only alienate people," they said. "This will come back to haunt you." At first I was surprised by what felt like a dramatic overreaction. But I soon realized why I had fallen out of sync with the

progressive mainstream on the use of the R-words: I had been spending time listening to and reading evangelical Christians who are preaching revolution.

Exley's blog, "Revolution in Jesusland," has followed his pilgrimage across America to communities that embody this spirit of demonstrating the kingdom of God—not just for themselves in the transcendent "then and there," but also for others in the immanent "here and now." He represents many people who otherwise would write off Christianity who instead are ready to give the gospel another hearing (or perhaps better, viewing). They realize that salvation is more than what the church had previously advertised.

## NOT REDEEMER ONLY

My quest to understand the gospel led me to the source of the gospel himself: Jesus Christ, the gospel incarnate. I began to realize that every articulation of the gospel I'd heard focused exclusively on Jesus Christ and his role as redeemer. Of course, it's true and good news that Jesus and his life and work function redemptively. But when we reduce Jesus to redeemer only, we miss another essential element of our faith: that Jesus is also creator.

The Gospel of John begins, "In the beginning was the Word, and the Word was with God, and the Word was God. He was with God in the beginning. Through him all things were made; without him nothing was made that has been made" (John 1:1-3). Likewise, in the hymn of Colossians 1:15-20, Paul affirms Jesus as both creator and redeemer. While verses 18-20 describe Jesus as redeemer, verses 15 and 16 confess him as creator: "He is the image of the invisible God, the firstborn over all creation. For by him all things were created: things in heaven and on earth, visible and invisible, whether thrones or powers or rulers or authorities; all things were created by him and for him."

I'm discovering that our postmodern world is consumed with questions of creation—even if they're not explicitly framed that way. We can hear these questions whenever our contemporaries ask, "What does it mean to be human, especially as more and more of life is influenced by and even dependent on technology?" "How do we understand gender and sexuality and how both are expressed?" "How do we live in an ecologically responsible way?" "How might a just economy function sustainably?"

Have you had these conversations? Have you talked to the teenagers among you who verbalize these concerns? These are the questions our culture is wrestling with.

A reduced version of the gospel will have little to say to such questions. No wonder so many people have determined that the church and "the gospel" have very little to contribute to the world. The idea that the gospel has something to say about the eternal destinies of people has been drummed into them for a long time. But they don't see that we're equally concerned about what Jesus taught us to pray: "your kingdom come, your will be done on earth as it is in heaven" (Matthew 6:10).

People aren't asking the traditional gospel question much anymore. Asking, "If I died tomorrow, where would I end up?" doesn't generate much life. But asking people, "If you had just a few years left, what kind of life would you want to live?" generates enormous energy. This is a question of hope, something our balkanized world sorely needs.

And perhaps not surprisingly, Jesus has a response to those who ask this question and who find themselves on this quest. To them he says, "Wake up. . . . The kingdom of God is at hand. . . . Come, follow me."

# God's Cure for Heart Trouble

*Christ waits to bring salvation to those*
*who eagerly wait for him.*

by Greg Laurie

After reading a *Time* magazine cover story on the topic of fear, I discovered a lot of fears I didn't even know existed. These are actual phobias that some Americans have:

kathisophobia: the fear of sitting

ablutophobia: the fear of bathing

dentophobia: fear of dentists

cyclophobia: the fear of bicycles

alektorophobia: the fear of chickens

arachibutyrophobia: the fear of peanut butter sticking to the roof of your mouth

automatonophobia: the fear of ventriloquist dummies

peladophobia—the fear of baldness or bald people

phobophobia—the fear of phobias!

A lot of things worry us and fill us with stress. Life is filled with troubles. Job 5:7 says, "Yet man is born to trouble."

Life is filled with many disappointments. Maybe you had certain goals set for yourself when you were younger, but you've never reached those goals. Maybe you wanted to be a better person, but you fell short. Maybe you wanted to be more successful, but you've had many failures. Maybe you wanted to be loved, but people often seem indifferent toward you.

Circumstances can also be a source of trouble. Maybe you've had some bad news recently. Perhaps you were laid off. Maybe you have some kind of illness. Maybe there are problems at home right now.

I want to share with you the words Jesus gave 2,000 years ago to stressed-out, agitated people. These words are God's cure for heart trouble: "'Do not let your hearts be troubled. Trust in God; trust also in me. In my Father's house are many rooms; if it were not so, I would have told you. I am going there to prepare a place for you. And if I go and prepare a place for you, I will come back and take you to be with me that you also may be where I am. You know the way to the place where I am going.' Thomas said to him, 'Lord, we don't know where you are going, so how can we know the way?' Jesus answered, 'I am the way and the truth and the life. No one comes to the Father except through me'" (John 14:1-6).

Why were the disciples afraid when Jesus offered these words to them? Part of the reason was that he'd just dropped a number of bombshells on them. He revealed that one of the Twelve would betray him. He also told them that Simon Peter—regarded as the ringleader of the disciples—would deny him. Then he gave the worst news of all: he was going to leave them.

At this point, the disciples didn't understand that Jesus came to this earth with the express purpose of going to the cross, dying for the sin of the world, and then rising from the dead. They thought he would establish an earthly kingdom. When he said, "I'm going to leave you," it freaked them out. That's why Jesus went on to say, "Do not let your hearts be troubled." Essentially, he was saying: "Even when it seems like your world is falling apart and darkness is going to overtake you, you don't need to feel anxious or worried."

Jesus offered the disciples three reasons why they didn't have to worry, and the same principles apply to us in our agitated, stress-filled world today. Let's look at each of Jesus' cures for heart trouble.

## TAKE GOD AT HIS WORD

Jesus' first direction about not worrying was to take God at his word. Jesus began by saying, "Believe in me." When you become a Christian—when you admit to God that you're a sinner and ask Jesus Christ to come into your heart to be your Savior and Lord—God takes residence inside you and begins to reveal to you his plan for your life. No more accidents. You're not merely a victim of fate, hoping that your luck doesn't run out. Now you're a child of God, under his divine protection. And the word "oops" isn't in God's vocabulary. God gives us the user's manual of life. I love gadgets. I visit all the gadget websites and read all the gadget magazines. I want to know about the new digital camera that has even more megapixels than the last one. I want more storage; I want more memory; I want a faster CPU. I like all that stuff. But here's the problem: I hate to read manuals.

In the same way, as Christians, we often ignore the user's manual for life—the Bible. God tells us how to live, the purpose of life, and, most importantly, how to get to heaven. The Bible tells me certain things I shouldn't do, and certain things I should do if I want to live a life that is full and meaningful. If God tells you not to do something, it's for your own good. The Bible says, "No good thing does [God] withhold from those whose walk is blameless" (Psalm 84:11). He tells you what to do to live a life that will have meaning and purpose.

The Bible says, "All Scripture is inspired by God" (2 Timothy 3:16, *NASB*). It teaches us what's true and makes us realize what's wrong in our lives. It straightens us out and teaches us to do what's right. So why should we not be filled with stress and agitation and fear? Because God's Word is true!

## TRUST WE'RE GOING TO HEAVEN

The second reason we don't need to have troubled hearts is God offers us the gift of heaven. Jesus said, "In My Father's house are many dwelling places" (John 14:2, *NASB*). Of course, this only holds true for those who put their faith in Jesus Christ.

I know that when I die, I'll go to heaven. That's not a boast. I'm not better than anyone else—but I am better off than someone who hasn't put his faith in Christ. I'm just one beggar telling another beggar where to find food. Because I've put my faith in Jesus, I know that when I die, I will go to heaven. God gives this promise to me and all who put their faith in Christ. When I die, I'll immediately go into the presence of the Lord. No matter what happens to you on this earth as a Christian, it pales when compared with this great hope. The apostle Paul wrote, "For our present troubles are quite small and won't last very long. Yet they produce for us an immeasurably great glory that will last forever!" (2 Corinthians 4:17, *NLT*). We don't look at the troubles we see right now, but we look forward to what we'll have that isn't yet seen. The troubles we see will soon be over. But the joys that come will last forever. Deep down inside, we all long for a place we've never been. C. S. Lewis called this the "inconsolable longing." He wrote: "There have been times when I think we do not desire heaven; but more often I find myself wondering whether, in our heart of hearts, we have ever desired anything else. . . . It is the secret signature of each soul, the incommunicable and unappeasable want, the thing we desired before we met our wives or made our friends or chose our work, and which we will still desire on our deathbed, when the mind no longer knows wife or friend or work" (C. S. Lewis, *The Problem of Pain*).

We all long for something more, sensing within that more exists to this life.

Remember how much I love gadgets? They're so cool when you first get them! You think, Oh, this is so hot. This is the latest, newest thing. Then your buddy comes along and he's got a newer gadget that just came out. All of a sudden, your gadget isn't so cool. We always think, Oh, if I just had this, I know I would be happy. If I were married to this woman, or this man, or if I lived in this house, or if I drove this car, or if I had this position—then I would be happy. But then you find yourself in that position—you get the car, the person, or whatever it is—and you say, "Well, I don't know. Maybe it's this other thing."

We're always searching, because we're hardwired to know God. We're hardwired to know there's more to life. That "inconsolable longing" is to intimately know God.

## JESUS IS COMING BACK

The third reason we don't need to let our hearts be troubled is because Jesus Christ is coming back again.

Newspapers have a certain type they save only for mega-events. They used it when President Kennedy was assassinated in Dallas, when Pearl Harbor was bombed, and on the day after the attacks on the World Trade Center and the Pentagon. It's the kind of type that grabs you by the throat and it says, "Read me!" They don't call it "big news" type or "major event" type. They call it "Second Coming" type, because no bigger event exists than the Second Coming of Jesus Christ.

Jesus said, "I will come again and receive you to Myself" (John 14:3, *NASB*). Christ will be coming back for those who are watching and waiting. Hebrews 9:28 says that Jesus will come again, but not to deal with our sins. This time, he will come and bring salvation to those who eagerly wait for him. Are you ready for the return of Jesus? The Bible says he will come in a moment—in the twinkling of an eye—and we will be "caught up . . . to meet the Lord in the air" (1 Thessalonians 4:17, *NLT*). Jesus said that two will be in a field—one will be taken and the other left. Two will be in a bed—one will be taken and the other left (Luke 17:34-36). He was speaking of that moment when he comes for his people. Will you be ready to meet the Lord? Jesus said to the disciples, "And you know the way where I am going" (John 14:4, *NASB*). Most of the disciples were probably nodding and saying, "Absolutely!" But not Thomas! Thomas said: "Excuse me, but I have a question. We don't know where you're going, and we don't know the way."

Aren't you glad Thomas asked that question? I'm glad, because it caused our Lord to respond: "I am the way, and the truth, and the life; no one comes to the Father but through Me" (John 14:6, *NASB*). This statement is one of the most controversial aspects of our faith, because we're saying that Jesus is the only way to a relationship with God. Some people don't believe that. A Barna poll revealed that half of all Americans believe if a person is generally good and does enough good things for others during their life, he'll earn a place in heaven. That's a nice thought, but it's not what the Bible says. Not only that, whose definition of good would we use? If you operate by this concept, as 54 percent of Americans do, you need to do more good deeds in your life than bad deeds. Do you honestly think you've done more good than bad? I'd suggest that very few of us have! Most of us fall far short of that standard.

Of course, that's not the standard God will judge us by. One sin is enough to keep us out of heaven. The Bible says that if you offend in one point of the law, you're guilty of all of it (James 2:10). That means that every one of us has sinned over and over again.

What is sin? Sin means to cross a line—to trespass. You've seen the signs at the park: "Do Not Trespass" or "Don't Step on the Grass." Sin is like crossing a line you're not supposed to cross. The word also means "to fall short of." God set a high standard for all of humanity—absolute perfection—and not one of us measures up to that standard. We all fall short.

You might be asking, "If that's true, how will I ever get right with God?" Answer: You won't—apart from Jesus Christ. God loved you so much that he sent his Son 2,000 years ago. Jesus was more than a good man. He was the God-man, fully God and fully man. He was born in a manger in Bethlehem, lived a perfect life, died the perfect death, rose again from the dead three days later, and now stands at the door of your life. He knocks and says, "If you will hear my voice and open the door, I will come in" (Revelation 3:20, author paraphrase). You might think: I don't like that. It's such a narrow approach. But it's the truth.

Here's an analogy that might help us better understand. Let's say you're on a plane to Hawaii. You're taxiing down the runway. You've got your seat-belt on. You've turned off your electronic devices. You then hear the voice of the pilot as you're beginning your ascent: "Good morning, ladies and gentle-men. Welcome to flight 1492 with service to Honolulu, Hawaii. Our cruising altitude will be 32,000 feet, and we'll be showing a movie." You think, That sounds good. But then you hear the pilot make this statement: "By the way, folks, I'm not so sure about this whole fuel thing. I see that the gauge indicates we don't have enough fuel to reach our destination, but don't worry about it. I feel really good about this. I have all these navigation devices, but I'm not going to use any of them. I feel that's too narrow and bigoted. Folks, I believe that all roads lead to Hawaii. By the way, I'm very sincere about this." You'd think, We have a lunatic in the cockpit!

Interestingly, in the most important issue of all—where we're going to spend eternity—we'll take this loose view: "I think as long as a person is sincere and believes something with all of his heart, that's good enough." Well, it isn't. We all fall short of God's glory (Romans 3:23). We all need his forgiveness, and Jesus offers it. . . .

You can know that you'll go to heaven when you die. You'll know that you'll be ready for the Lord's return.

© Greg Laurie. Used with permission. This article was adapted from a sermon by Greg Laurie and was originally published on Preaching Today Audio or PreachingToday.com, resources of Christianity Today International.

# The New Testament: Fact or Fiction?

*The New Testament is a reliable, historical document.*

by Steve May

In college I had a job where I was given the nickname "Sleeping Beauty." It wasn't because I overslept, and it certainly wasn't because of my looks. I got the name when one of my co-workers, an avid non-Christian, found out that I was going into the ministry. He said to me, "I can't believe that you believe that fairy tale! I thought you were intelligent!" He went on to say, "You're just a regular Sleeping Beauty, aren't you?" And the name stuck. What my co-worker didn't know was that I'd already spent months and months struggling with questions about my faith. I asked myself that question: Is Christianity nothing more than an elaborate fairy tale? How do I know the Bible is God's Word? How do I know the Gospels—the stories of the life of Jesus—weren't embellished over the years to the point of becoming filled with myths and legends that never really took place? How do I know that Jesus is the Son of God? What about the intellectual objections to Christianity? When I started asking these questions, I'd been a

Christian for about five years. My faith consisted primarily of believing what I'd been told to believe. Eventually, I realized that wasn't good enough. I didn't want to spend the rest of my life having my faith spoon-fed to me. So, I began asking some hard questions. During this time I never renounced my faith or turned my back on Christianity—I just wanted to be sure of what I believed. I realized that if Christianity is true, it will stand up under scrutiny. So I began to read everything I could on the subject. Over time, I became convinced that the Bible is the Word of God, Jesus is the Son of God, and that following him is the most intelligent thing a person can do.

So when my friends called me "Sleeping Beauty," I couldn't help but laugh, because by then I knew that Christianity is more than just a fairy tale. I knew beyond a doubt that Christianity is all that it claims to be.

That was 20 years ago, and I'm still just as convinced today. Let's take a look at the New Testament and explore why it's a reliable document.

## SEEKING THE TRUTH

Let's consider some crucial questions about the New Testament: When the Gospels tell the story of the life, death, and resurrection of Jesus, can you trust them? When you read the stories of Jesus, are you reading fairy tales or are you reading facts? An overwhelming amount of evidence supports the credibility of the New Testament—so I want to list three reasons why I believe the Bible. If you have questions about Christianity, or questions about the authority of the Bible, this article will give you some answers. If you still have questions, keep asking. Keep looking. Keep seeking. Jesus said, "You will know the truth, and the truth will set you free" (John 8:32). You don't have to be afraid to ask questions, because you don't have to be afraid of the truth. It will set you free. So, keep asking until you're convinced. One of the questions I used to ask is, "Can I really trust the New Testament?" As

I sought the answer to this question, I discovered at least three reasons why I can trust the New Testament.

## IT'S HISTORICALLY RELIABLE

Did you read Homer's *Iliad* in high school or college? Most of us did—or we at least read the Cliff Notes. Homer's *Iliad* has the greatest manuscript authority of any non-Christian ancient work. Some 650 ancient manuscripts of *Iliad* survive; the earliest dates back to the third century. *Iliad* was written in 650 B.C., meaning a 1,000-year span exists between the time it was written and the earliest surviving manuscript. Aristotle's *Poetics* was written in 343 B.C. The earliest manuscript in existence is dated 1100 A.D. That's a span of about 1,400 years. Caesar's *History of the Gallic Wars* was written around 50 B.C. There are less than a dozen existing manuscripts of this work; the oldest dates back to the ninth century A.D. That's a span of about 1,000 years. Tacitus wrote *The Annals of Imperial Rome* in 116 A.D. The earliest manuscript for this work dates back to 850 A.D. That's a span of about 700 years. Historians consider these works to be authoritative and reliable even though they're copies of copies of copies—hundreds of years newer than the originals. Why? Because scholars have learned that copies can be trusted. In ancient times, copyists took their job seriously and were meticulous about accuracy. For example, archaeologists have found copies of *Iliad* in different parts of the world that are virtually identical to one another.

Of course, the more copies of a piece of historical literature that exist, the better. The New Testament is unique in that we know of more than 20,000 ancient New Testament manuscripts, with the earliest fragments dating back to the second century. Other ancient writings also contain countless references to various books of the New Testament. For example, in 95 A.D. Clement of Rome wrote a letter to the church in Corinth, and in that letter he quotes from or refers to Matthew, Luke, Romans, Corinthians, Hebrews, 1 Timothy, and 1 Peter.

Polycarp wrote a letter to the church of Philippi in 110 A.D., and quotes from 10 of Paul's letters and from 1 Peter. The *Didache*, an early church document written between 80 and 120 A.D., contains 22 quotations from Matthew, and includes references to Luke, John, Acts, Romans, and 1 Peter.

These are just a few examples that demonstrate that the books of the New Testament were written and widely circulated throughout the first century.

The oldest New Testaments books, 1 Thessalonians and Galatians, were both written by the apostle Paul around 49 A.D. The oldest Gospel, Mark, was written around 55–60 A.D. Some people might say, "Wait a minute! That's 25 years after the death of Jesus! That's a long time! In 25 years, a lot of myth and legend can be added to a story." However, that's not true. Even 25 years after Jesus' death, thousands and thousands of people in Jerusalem who had been alive at the time of Christ would still remember the events surrounding his life, death, and resurrection.

If the Gospels contained embellished or fabricated stories, these witnesses could have and would have publicly disputed what had been written about Jesus. Remember, at this time, many powerful people despised Christianity and wanted nothing more than for this crazy cult to go away. If the facts presented in the Gospels were anything less than common knowledge, this literature never would have become widely distributed. But they were widely distributed—throughout Jerusalem, Judea, Asia Minor, Egypt, and Africa. They were copied countless times and translated into a number of different languages. Based on the number of ancient manuscripts available, the New Testament is obviously a book to be taken seriously.

Dr. Clark Pinnock, a professor of systematic theology at McMasters University, wrote: "There exists no document from the ancient world witnessed by so excellent a set of textual and historical testimonies . . . on which an intelligent decision may be made. An honest person cannot dismiss a source of this kind. Skepticism regarding the historical credentials of Christianity is based upon an irrational bias."

## IT HAS PASSED THE TEST OF TIME

We can also trust the New Testament because it has stood the test of time. The New Testament contains 27 books. Do you know how we got them? As a new Christian, I was surprised to learn that dozens of Christian writings existed in the early days of the church that were considered for inclusion in the New Testament, but didn't make the final cut. For example, the Gospel according to Thomas, the Gospel according to Peter, the Acts of Paul, the Epistle of Barnabas, the Shepherd of Hermas, the Apocalypse of Peter, the Apocalypse of Stephen, the Acts of Andrew, the Gospel of Nicodemus, and on and on.

I wondered: Why weren't these books included in the Bible? The Gospel of Peter—shouldn't that have been in there? I mean, after all, Peter walked on water! And the Acts of Paul? Paul might be the most significant person in church history. Shouldn't this book have been included? And who decided what to include, anyway?

To answer the last question first, in 397 A.D. the Council of Carthage convened and officially determined which books would and would not be included in the New Testament. This council, consisting of church leaders from throughout the world, didn't just arbitrarily choose 27 books. They chose books already commonly accepted throughout the world to be Scripture. As early as the first century, church leaders began compiling lists of the most authoritative books in an effort to establish a Christian Bible.

During the time that Paul, Peter, John, Luke, Matthew, and Mark wrote the books of the New Testament, other people wrote books and letters about

Jesus, too. Some of these writings were immediately recognized as authoritative. Some were recognized as valuable, but weren't accepted throughout the entire church. And some were recognized to be, as a fourth-century church historian said, totally absurd. For example, a book called the Gospel of Nicodemus was immediately disputed for a couple of reasons: First, no evidence existed that Nicodemus actually wrote it. And second, it contained stories and sayings about Jesus that weren't part of the well-known oral tradition, and as a result were seen as fabrications. The same could be said of the Gospel of Peter: There was no evidence that Peter had written it, and it contained sayings attributed to Jesus that weren't consistent with what the more authoritative books taught about Jesus. It became obvious that these books—and others like them—weren't authentic and didn't belong in the New Testament.

The New Testament didn't come together because one man simply decided one day that these books would be in the New Testament. The development of the New Testament was a 300-year process, during which hundreds of leaders of the early church recognized the value of these writings. Through their wisdom and their scholarship—and with the guidance of the Holy Spirit—they determined what was authentic and what wasn't.

The books of the New Testament didn't just accidentally fall into place. These books proved themselves to the early church leaders to be the Word of God. Also, when I read Scripture, I remind myself that throughout history thousands of people have died for this book. Yet, the Bible itself lives on. It has passed the test of time.

## IT WORKS!

I also believe the New Testament is authentic because for the last 25 years it has been my goal to live according to the principles of this book. There have been times when I have failed to live up to that standard, and I regret it every single time. But I've learned a simple truth: When I live according to the teachings of the Bible, my life works. That doesn't mean my life has always been easy—because sometimes obedience is the hardest path to follow. But when I live according to the principles taught in Scripture, I experience the presence and power of God in my life.

The apostle Paul wrote, "All Scripture is inspired by God and is useful to teach us what is true and to make us realize what is wrong in our lives. It straightens us out and teaches us to do what is right. It is God's way of preparing us in every way, fully equipped for every good thing God wants us to do" (2 Timothy 3:16, 17, *NLT*).

Consider just a couple of ways the Bible works in our lives the way Paul described:

The Bible teaches us what is true. You'll find a message in the Bible that isn't taught anywhere else in the world.

It teaches that God loves you, that Jesus died for you, that you can be forgiven, that God's mercy is greater than any sin, that there is life, and power, and healing in the name of Jesus.

It teaches that if you give your life to Jesus, you'll be filled with the presence of God and experience peace that passes all understanding.

It teaches that this world belongs to God, that the future belongs to him, that he is Lord over all creation, and that someday every knee will bow and every tongue will confess that Jesus Christ is Lord.

The Bible makes us realize what's wrong in our lives. Long ago, I decided that I wouldn't let the world or any individual in the world define my concept of right and wrong. Other people will try to make you feel guilty for the craziest things, and at the same time will make excuses for destructive behavior. A friend of mine involved in a hunger relief project told me about a meeting he attended. They were having snacks when one of the other members said, "It's a sin to eat potato chips when so many in the world are hungry." Of course, the Bible clearly says we do need to help the poor and the hungry. But the Bible doesn't teach that it's a sin to enjoy a potato chip every once in a while. The world has no clue about right and wrong. In one ear you'll be told to look out for number one and let the other guy fend for himself; in the other ear you're told that it's a sin to eat potato chips. The Bible puts an end to that confusion. It tells us where we're wrong. It convicts us of sin. We can look to it for guidance. That's why the writer of Hebrews wrote: "For the word of God is living and active. Sharper than any double-edged sword, it penetrates even to dividing soul and spirit, joints and marrow; it judges the thoughts and attitudes of the heart" (Hebrews 4:12).

God's Word straightens us out and teaches us to do what is right. It teaches us to turn our back on sin; it teaches us how to love; it teaches us how to give; it teaches us how to forgive; it teaches us how to treat others; it teaches us how to raise our children; it teaches us how to walk with Christ. It teaches us to do what is right.

I believe in the Bible because it works. When I read: "Do not be anxious about anything, but in everything, by prayer and petition, with thanksgiving, present your requests to God. And the peace of God, which transcends all understanding, will guard your hearts and your minds in Christ Jesus" (Philippians 4:6, 7), I know that verse really works!

When the Bible says: "Trust in the LORD with all your heart and lean not on your own understanding; in all your ways acknowledge him, and he will make your paths straight" (Proverbs 3:5, 6), I can be confident that verse really works!

When the Bible says: "Ask and it will be given to you; seek and you will find; knock and the door will be opened to you" (Matthew 7:7), I'm certain this verse really works!

I could go on and on and on, reciting verse after verse. The most powerful proof for the reliability of the New Testament can be found in the fact that it works. It delivers what it promises.

## CONCLUSION

Regardless of what someone told you in college, or what you've heard some skeptic say, the New Testament is a reliable, historical document. It tells the story of the life, death, and resurrection of Jesus—an account told by eyewitnesses. It spread like wildfire throughout the known world because the story was too powerful to be refuted.

The New Testament didn't come into existence because one person—or even a handful of people—decided which books would be in the New Testament. Thousands of faithful Christians over a period of hundreds of years attested to the authority of these writings. This is a book that many people have given their lives for. Why? Because it works. If you read it, believe it, and apply it to your life, you'll never be the same.

# FIND SPIRITUAL FORMATION TOOLS
## at Christian BibleStudies.com

▶ Join over **125,000 people** who use ChristianBibleStudies.com

▶ Choose from **over 800 downloadable Bible studies** to find exactly what you're looking for

▶ Study through a book of the Bible **verse-by-verse**, discuss an important topic from Scripture, or learn about **hot topics** like movies and politics

▶ Pay only once and make up to **1,000 copies**

▶ Enhance your personal devotions, small groups, or Sunday School classes

▶ Facilitate **lively discussions** with fascinating topics

a service of

## CHRISTIANITY TODAY
INTERNATIONAL

# BUILD AN EFFECTIVE MINISTRY with Small Groups.com

Inspiring
Life-Changing
Community

▶ Learn how to **start or re-start** both small groups and entire ministries

▶ Choose from thousands of **training tools, Bible studies, and free articles** from trusted leaders like Philip Yancey, Les and Leslie Parrott, and Larry Crabb

▶ Connect your group with a free and fun **social-networking tool**

▶ **Train yourself and your leaders** with invaluable assessments and orientation guides

▶ Downloadable resources are ready for **immediate use** and can be copied up to 1,000 times

▶ Join the **blog conversation** and share your small-group experiences

a service of

CHRISTIANITY TODAY
INTERNATIONAL

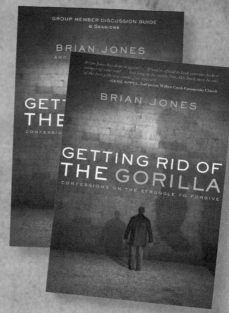